THE ELECTRONIC RESOURCES TROUBLESHOOTING GUIDE

ALA Editions purchases fund advocacy, awareness, and accreditation programs for library professionals worldwide.

THE ELECTRONIC RESOURCES TROUBLESHOOTING GUIDE

HOLLY TALBOTT AND **ASHLEY ZMAU**

CHICAGO 2020

Holly Talbott has more than six years of experience with electronic resources and is coauthor of *Electronic Resources Librarianship: A Practical Guide for Librarians* (Rowman & Littlefield, 2018). She is the electronic resources librarian at Kent State University and was previously the electronic resources and licensing librarian at the University of Arizona Libraries and the electronic resources librarian at Lasell College.

Ashley Zmau has more than ten years of academic library experience and is coauthor of *Electronic Resources Librarianship: A Practical Guide for Librarians* (Rowman & Littlefield, 2018). She is the serials cataloger for the Dallas County Community College District and was previously the electronic resources librarian at the University of Texas at Arlington and the electronic resources management librarian at Southern Methodist University.

ISBNs
978-0-8389-4764-7 (paper)
978-0-8389-4791-3 (PDF)
978-0-8389-4793-7 (ePub)
978-0-8389-4792-0 (Kindle)

Library of Congress Cataloging-in-Publication Data
Names: Talbott, Holly, 1987- author. | Zmau, Ashley, 1988- author.
Title: The electronic resources troubleshooting guide / Holly Talbott and Ashley Zmau.
Description: Chicago : ALA Editions, 2020. | Includes bibliographical references and index.
  | Summary: "This guide shows you how to develop a library-wide workflow and a shared
  understanding of the components delivering electronic resources to your patrons"—
  Provided by publisher.
Identifiers: LCCN 2020010139 (print) | LCCN 2020010140 (ebook) | ISBN 9780838947647
  (paperback) | ISBN 9780838947913 (pdf) | ISBN 9780838947920 (kindle edition) |
  ISBN 9780838947937 (epub)
Subjects: LCSH: Libraries—Special collections—Electronic information resources. |
  Electronic information resources—Management. | Problem solving.
Classification: LCC Z692.C65 T354 2020 (print) | LCC Z692.C65 (ebook) | DDC
  025.17/4—dc23
LC record available at https://lccn.loc.gov/2020010139
LC ebook record available at https://lccn.loc.gov/2020010140

Cover design by Alejandra Diaz. Cover image © 1xpert.
Book design by Kim Thornton in the Laca and Chaparral Pro fonts.

♾ This paper meets the requirements of ANSI/NISO Z39.48-1992 (Permanence of Paper).

Printed in the United States of America
24 23 22 21 20   5 4 3 2 1

CONTENTS

PREFACE . . . vii

1 Troubleshooting as Problem Solving   1

2 The Access Chain   13

3 Soliciting Problem Reports   39

4 Diagnosing Access Issues   59

5 Resolving Access Issues   85

6 Common Access Issues and Examples   103

7 Troubleshooting Workflows and Training   125

8 Proactive Troubleshooting   157

CONCLUSION . . . 167

INDEX . . . 169

PREFACE

The Importance of Troubleshooting

Electronic resources are ubiquitous in libraries today. From e-books to open access journals, streaming videos to specialized content databases, libraries are relying more and more on electronic content to fill their patrons' information needs. In 2016, libraries worldwide spent an estimated 61 percent of their budgets on e-books, e-journals, databases, streaming media, and other online content (Publishers Communication Group 2017). That number is only expected to grow as the variety in content, purchase models, and availability of e-resources continues to proliferate.

Behind the scenes, librarians are busy stewarding this large portion of their budgets, carefully curating e-resources and ensuring their access and discoverability for patrons. However, with the volume and diversity of vendors, platforms, and access models, e-resources are susceptible to technology failures. These failures "have a direct and measurable impact on user experience, and the failure of those resources to perform reflects poorly on the library and the institution" (Wright 2016, 205). Therefore, establishing a strong troubleshooting workflow and staff, whose highest priority is customer service, is essential. With effective troubleshooting, a library can reduce patron frustration, foster a positive image of the library, increase the visibility of library services for patrons, and practice sound financial stewardship.

Unfortunately, as library systems continue to grow in number and complexity, librarians are often at a loss when confronted with sudden breaks in access, unsure what caused them, how to fix them, or where to turn for answers. In *The Electronic Resources Troubleshooting Guide,* we aim to fill this gap, equipping librarians with not only the knowledge and skills to diagnose and resolve access issues but also practical approaches for creating and maintaining effective workflows, recruiting and training staff across multiple departments, and making the most of their help ticket systems. Librarians will learn how to do the following:

- solicit problem reports
- conduct troubleshooting interviews
- recognize the symptoms of common access issues
- communicate with vendors and information technology (IT) personnel for speedy resolutions
- establish triage and troubleshooting workflows
- manage problem reports in either a commercial or a homegrown system
- train others to troubleshoot in a collaborative team environment

Structure of the Book

Chapter 1 lays the conceptual groundwork for the remainder of the book by discussing basic ideas of *problems* and *problem solving* upon which troubleshooting relies. We also explore the base attributes, skill sets, and infrastructure that directly influence how effective troubleshooters are in their work. By drawing on concepts outside the library science literature, we hope to jump-start your imagination to think differently about troubleshooting.

In chapters 2 through 6 we get technical, discussing the foundational systems knowledge necessary for designing and implementing an effective troubleshooting workflow. We begin with a thorough analysis of e-resource access chains before covering how to gather problem reports: what information to collect, how to conduct a troubleshooting interview, and how to work with both internal and external reporters throughout this process. We then move into problem diagnosis, focusing on the types and origins of metadata and how their utilization creates opportunities for failure within library systems. We end our technology section with a discussion on strategies to diagnose symptoms of common issues, as well as how to identify and handle systemic issues.

In chapters 7 and 8 we discuss project management, troubleshooting workflows, team troubleshooting, training others, and proactive troubleshooting. We speak at length about team troubleshooting, covering topics related to interpersonal dynamics, expectation management, and the involvement of non–troubleshooting team library staff members. Finally, we cover what you can learn from analyzing your library's problem reports and the various preventative maintenance routines that represent proactive troubleshooting.

Acting as a ready reference, *The Electronic Resources Troubleshooting Guide* will help librarians move beyond triage and temporary fixes by offering techniques for effective problem solving and proactively addressing access issues. With a little foresight and know-how, all librarians can feel confident when helping patrons, regardless of their positions or technology backgrounds.

REFERENCES

Publishers Communication Group (PCG). 2017. *Library Budget Predictions for 2017: Results from a Telephone Survey*. Boston, MA: PCG. www.pcgplus.com/wp-content/uploads/2017/05/Library-Budget-Predictions-for-2017-public.pdf.

Wright, Jennifer. 2016. "Electronic Outages: What Broke, Who Broke It, and How to Track It." *Library Resources and Technical Services* 60 (3): 204–13.

Troubleshooting as Problem Solving

Before we dive into the practicalities of troubleshooting library access issues, we must first establish some underlying concepts of problem solving and decision making, upon which the following chapters will rely. Troubleshooting, at its heart, is just a specialized form of problem solving. Regardless of whether you are trying to fix a broken link, start a stalled car, or make cost-efficient travel arrangements, the process of tackling and resolving a problem is the same. Furthermore, studies have shown that those who educate themselves on the problem-solving process and are able to articulate its various stages and strategies are likely to become more efficient, effective, and creative problem solvers—and, by extension, troubleshooters—than are those who rely on industry-specific knowledge alone (Gugerty 2007). For this reason, we dedicate the first half of this chapter to defining what constitutes a *problem* and *problem solving* and to outlining the general stages that make up the problem-solving process. We then pivot to troubleshooting in particular, focusing on the specific knowledge sets, organizational infrastructure, and attitudinal competencies that will set up a troubleshooter for success.

Defining a Problem

What is a problem? While intuitively we all know when we are experiencing a problem, articulating what, exactly, constitutes a problem can be a bit of a challenge. Scholars from across a broad spectrum of disciplines have worked to define problems and problem solving over the past several decades, with varying results. In his monograph on managerial decision making, George Huber (1980) defines a problem as the perceived contrast between a person's currently experienced situation and that person's desired situation—that is, "a difference between what we have and what we want" (12). Problem solving, then, is about reducing this difference, irrespective of the ease or difficulty in doing so. Michael Stevens, in contrast, considers a problem to be more than just goal attainment. In *Practical Problem Solving for Managers*, he defines a problem as a situation "in which we experience uncertainty or difficulty in achieving what we want to achieve" (Stevens and British Institute of Management 1988, 14). For him, a problem results from encountering an obstacle while in pursuit of an objective, not just by having an objective alone.

Stevens's view is much more in keeping with popular definitions of a problem in the disciplines of teaching and psychology. According to certain teaching theories, true problems, particularly in relation to mathematical tasks, must be *nonroutine* or *novel* to the solver and require the use of higher cognitive reasoning and thinking skills (Schoenfeld 1985; Lester and Kehle 2003; Francisco and Maher 2005). Situations that the solver has encountered before or whose solutions are readily obvious do not require the process of problem solving, merely the application of previously attained knowledge. Similarly, in cognitive psychology, a problem is said to exist when someone has a goal but does not know how to achieve it (Duncker 1945). Problem solving, then, is an exercise in knowledge attainment and decision making. If a situation's resolution is already known and just awaiting execution, a problem does not necessarily exist.

So where does that leave us? For the purposes of this book, we will be using Stevens's definition of a problem, which can be boiled down to this simple equation:

OBJECTIVE + OBSTACLE = PROBLEM

However, we have one modification. If we look closely at Stevens's full definition of a problem—"a situation in which we experience uncertainty or difficulty in achieving what we want to achieve" (Stevens and British Institute of Management 1988, 14)—we see that a problem is actually composed of three distinct elements: an objective, an obstacle, and a desire to overcome the obstacle to achieve the objective. This third, emotion-driven element is also present in the definitions of George Huber (1980) and Richard E. Mayer (2013), expressed implicitly through phrases like *has a goal*, *want to achieve*, and *desired situation*. Because each of these definitions starts from the premise that the objective is generated from within the problem solver—the manifestation of that person's own desires and aspirations—the motivation to overcome obstacles and achieve the objective is inherent to the situation. This is not necessarily true when it comes to troubleshooting.

Troubleshooting, especially within the context of a library work environment, is typically initiated by an outside source, such as a patron, coworker, or supervisor. It is the patron who has the goal and who has encountered the obstacle in pursuit of the goal. It is also the patron who harbors the desire to overcome the obstacle in order to achieve the objective. For example, a student may have the goal of obtaining a particular journal article that is critical to a research paper. However, the student encounters an obstacle when the necessary link within the library search interface leads to an error message. Becuase the student has a desire to overcome the obstacle and achieve the goal of obtaining the article, the student would begin the process of problem solving, which may include reaching out to the library staff, who, in turn, would attempt to resolve the problem for the student.

In such instances, library staff are taking on the objectives and desires of another individual, and thus making the individual's problem their own. (Or, if we want to be overly precise, we could say the library staff have the objective/desire to fulfill the individual's objective/desire—either because they wish to do their job well or they empathize with the individual or both—but this largely amounts to the same thing: taking on another person's problem as their own.) How fully library staff embrace the individual's objective will naturally affect how much energy they are willing to expend overcoming any obstacles that are encountered. More invested staff members will likely be more inclined to learn and engage in extensive problem-solving behaviors, while less invested staff members may expend minimal effort, give up if the answer is not readily obvious, or not even think a problem exists at all. In other words, it is this third, emotion-driven motivational element that determines whether and to what degree a troubleshooter will acknowledge a problem exists and engage in the problem-solving process.

Thus, taking these three elements into consideration, we can define a problem as follows:

OBJECTIVE + OBSTACLE + MOTIVATION (to overcome obstacle) = PROBLEM

The Two Problems of Library Troubleshooting

Within the library, access issues are typically composed of two distinct problems. The first, which we alluded to earlier, is patron focused. In our example, the problem was that a student was unable to access the article needed for a research paper. Here, the objective of the troubleshooter is to provide the patron with access to the article, despite the obstacle of the interface link being broken. Once the article has come into the patron's possession, the problem—at least from the patron's perspective—ceases to exist. This, of course, opens the door to a lot of potential solutions, many of which have nothing to do with fixing the broken link. However, it is unlikely many troubleshooters would consider the access issue truly resolved while the link remains broken. This is because of the second problem, which is technology focused. The goal for the troubleshooter is to have a system that functions as it is intended, with a problem arising only when an obstacle—sometimes known, sometimes unknown—causes the system to behave incorrectly. Once the obstacle is identified and removed and the system returns to its properly functioning state, the problem is resolved.

In many cases, a troubleshooter will need to solve both the patron-focused problem and the technology-focused problem to successfully resolve an access issue. Such is the case for our previous example: the troubleshooter would need to both obtain access to the article for the patron and fix the broken link. However, problems can exist singly as well, with either the patron or the technology being the focal point. For example, in instances of user error, a patron may discover a citation within the discovery system but believe it should also link to the full text. The system is still functioning as it should; however, because the patron is not knowledgeable in using the system, the patron may report the full text as missing. In such cases, the access issue can be resolved by assisting the patron in retrieving the full text through another method, such as interlibrary loan. No adjustment to the system would be necessary. On the flip side, an access issue may present itself when library staff members are performing a routine check of their database A–Z list and uncover a broken link, which was otherwise not reported. The solution to this problem is purely technological. Once the librarian discovers and updates the broken URL within the database A–Z list, the problem is resolved.

The Stages of Problem Solving

Keeping in mind the definition of a *problem* and the two types of problems that troubleshooting needs to address, let's turn our attention to the problem-solving process itself. Quickly defined, problem solving is the mental processes involved in overcoming an obstacle to achieve an objective. These mental processes are generally divided into four stages (Pólya 1945):

1. *Understanding the problem:* During this stage, the problem solver endeavors to fully understand the problem, including its root cause.
2. *Evaluating options and planning the solution:* During this stage, the problem solver explores the possible options for resolving the problem, including the resources (staff, time, effort) needed to implement them, and decides on a course of action.
3. *Implementing the solution:* During this stage, the problem solver carries out the solution.

4. *Monitoring/reviewing results:* During this stage, the problem solver determines whether the implemented solution fixed the problem; depending on the nature of the problem, continued monitoring may be required to ensure the problem is resolved; if the problem is not resolved, the problem solver may need to return to one or more of the previous stages.

While pursuing a solution, troubleshooters move through these four stages of problem solving whether they are aware of it or not; however, the path they follow is seldom as linear as the version just described. Instead, the process tends to be recursive, with troubleshooters revisiting previous stages to gather more information, brainstorm additional options, or try a new solution if their first proves to be ineffective. This type of looping behavior is both expected and, to a degree, desirable, particularly as the complexity of the problem and the system in which it resides increases; however, too much time spent revisiting previous stages is also inefficient. By bringing the problem-solving process into their conscious awareness, troubleshooters are able to fully think through each of the stages, which, in turn, reduces the amount of time spent backtracking due to faulty assumptions, errors, or poorly conceived diagnoses and resolution strategies. This is especially true for novice troubleshooters who are less familiar with the system and, therefore, more prone to these errors.

We wanted to expand upon this process and identify a methodology that takes into consideration the needs and best practices particular to troubleshooting access issues in a library environment—specifically, the needs around communication, assessment, and documentation. Several expanded troubleshooting methodologies already exist within the discipline of information technology, including the six-step methodology recommended by CompTIA, the Computing Technology Industry Association, and the DECSAR method, which was first developed by Craig Ross in 2004 to assist in the education and training of novice troubleshooters. The DECSAR method in particular is notable for its depiction of the iterative nature of troubleshooting. This method identifies both the ideal linear path, which is often the sole focus of other troubleshooting methodologies, and the backtracking, or recursive thinking, that is necessary depending on the complexity of the issue and the skill of the troubleshooter. The DECSAR method is also highly generalizable—something Craig Ross and R. Robert Orr (2009) noted about the improved results of the office administration professionals who were trained in the method—and as a result has gained in popularity outside of information technology, including among librarians looking to augment their and their staffs' troubleshooting skills.

For this book, we use a modified version of Ross's DECSAR method that consists of these seven stages:

1. Identify and define the problem.
2. Examine the situation.
3. Consider the possible causes.
4. Consider the possible solutions.
5. Implement the solution.
6. Review the results.
7. Communicate and document the resolution.

We have organized our instructional content according to this seven-stage methodology. In chapter 3, we tackle the first two stages, exploring ways to effectively gather the information needed to understand the patron-focused and technology-focused problems. In chapter 4, we focus on diagnosis and pinpointing the possible causes of technological malfunctions. We cover solutions and their implementation, including how to communicate and document the resolution for others, in chapter 5. Finally, in chapter 6, we walk through the seven-stage method in its entirety as we look at some common access issues and their resolutions.

Keys to Effective Troubleshooting

Now that we have explored the concepts of problems and problem solving in relation to troubleshooting, let's focus more specifically on the various factors that influence its success. A troubleshooter's effectiveness is dependent on a mixture of general-purpose strategy, technical expertise, a well-functioning infrastructure and workflow, and attitudinal competencies. Some of these factors—such as troubleshooting strategies, technical expertise, and general attitude—are within a troubleshooter's ability to modify or control. Other factors—such as organizational leadership, well-functioning workflows, and infrastructure—may or may not be. In this section, we introduce each of these factors and their importance to troubleshooting. We discuss them in more depth in later chapters, focusing on specific suggestions and strategies for improvement.

GENERAL AND DOMAIN-SPECIFIC KNOWLEDGE

Beyond understanding and mastering the basics of problem solving, troubleshooters need to develop both general-purpose troubleshooting skills and domain-specific technical knowledge. General-purpose troubleshooting skills are those skills which "are applicable in diverse domains" in the sense that "they can be applied in any troubleshooting domain, including medical diagnosis, computer program debugging, and electronic troubleshooting" (Gugerty 2007, 135–36). In other words, they are transferable strategies that can be used to troubleshoot many kinds of technologies across a diverse spectrum of industries.

One well-known, general-purpose method of troubleshooting is trial and error. Using this strategy, the troubleshooter tries various solutions at random until happening to select the correct answer. For example, in the case of an unknown PIN (personal identification number), a person may try punching in numbers at random until stumbling upon the right sequence. Or, similarly, if faced with an unresponsive computer, a person may try multiple approaches at random—like rebooting, unplugging, or recharging the computer—in the hopes of unfreezing it. As you can imagine, the trial-and-error method of troubleshooting is highly inefficient and impractical for complex systems, like those encountered in a library. As such, it is typically used when the troubleshooter in question is a novice or lacks technical knowledge of the system (Jonassen and Hung 2006).

For this book, we employ several widely used, general troubleshooting strategies:

Elimination: Using this method, the troubleshooter isolates the cause of the issue by systematically testing and eliminating possible causes; similar to trial and error, this method becomes more impractical as the system increases in complexity.

Backtracking: Using this method, the troubleshooter isolates the cause of the issue by starting at the point of system failure and reasoning backward, testing each possible cause along the way (Gugerty 2007).

Re-creation: Using this method, the troubleshooter isolates the cause of the issue by finding a procedure (sequence of steps or events) that consistently induces the symptoms/failure to occur.

Half-splitting: Using this method, the troubleshooter divides the system into portions (traditionally halves) and checks each portion for symptoms of the issue; this procedure is repeated in the portion where the symptoms occur (by again dividing and testing each half) until the cause of the issue has been isolated; this strategy is efficient when a system is complex and "appears to contain several potential faults with no strong indication of where the actual fault lies" (Jonassen 2010, 85).

Just like with problem solving, learning general-purpose troubleshooting skills improves a troubleshooter's ability to quickly diagnose and resolve access issues; however, these skills cannot be used without a deep understanding of the technical system the troubleshooter is working within. This technical knowledge, often referred to as domain-specific knowledge, is the single biggest differentiator in competency between a novice and an expert troubleshooter (Gugerty 2007; Schaafstal, Schraagen, and van Berl 2000). The importance of building a troubleshooter's technical knowledge, therefore, cannot be overstated.

In an article for the *Journal of Electronic Resources Librarianship*, Sunshine Carter and Stacie Traill (2017) identify ten essential skills and knowledge for library access troubleshooting, six of which are specific categories of technical information:

- overview of discovery and access environment
- authentication and authorization
- OpenURL and link resolvers
- discovery index, activations, and linking mechanisms
- metadata quality, resources, and impact on access
- detailed interaction between link resolver, discovery index, discovery layer, and learning management system (LMS)

This list is not exhaustive—a point Carter and Traill readily acknowledge in their article—which speaks to the complex and unstandardized nature of library systems. Each library will need to identify its own essential knowledge for access troubleshooting based on its locally implemented systems, needs, and pain points. In chapters 2 through 5 of this book, we cover what we consider to be the basics of essential access troubleshooting knowledge, but please keep in mind your local needs as you assess the information provided in these chapters.

ATTITUDINAL COMPETENCIES

Effective troubleshooting requires more than just an application of technical knowledge and troubleshooting strategies. Intangible personal qualities, such as emotional and motivational traits, directly influence a troubleshooter's capabilities. As Richard E. Mayer (1998) states, "a focus solely on teaching problem solving skill and metaskill is incomplete, because it ignores the problem solver's feelings and interest in the problem" (50). Although many emotional factors can play a role in troubleshooting, we have found motivation, curiosity, and cognitive flexibility to be the most influential.

As mentioned previously in this chapter, a problem is composed of three factors: an objective, an obstacle, and the desire to overcome the obstacle in order to achieve the objective. This third element—motivation—is crucial to successful problem solving because it dictates how much time and effort an individual is willing to devote to overcoming the obstacle. The greater the motivation, the greater the lengths to which a troubleshooter will go to resolve an issue. Tenacity paired with technical knowledge makes for a very talented troubleshooter. Moreover, troubleshooters who are fully invested in seeing a problem through to its solution demonstrate the buy-in necessary to boost overall team morale, which, in turn, increases the efficacy of the entire team.

Similarly, skilled troubleshooters often possess an innate sense of curiosity about the systems and situations with which they work. This curiosity compels them to ask questions, seek out answers, and discover the *why* behind any given problem. It also directly impacts a troubleshooter's ability to adopt new strategies, deepen technical knowledge, and keep up with the ever-changing e-resource landscape—a necessity when cultivating a troubleshooter's resiliency.

In 2013, the North American Serials Interest Group released a list of core competencies for electronic resources librarians (NASIG, 2019). Among the competencies is a category of personal qualities that includes items like "flexibility," "open-mindedness," and a "high level of tolerance for complexity and ambiguity." These qualities fall under the umbrella term "cognitive flexibility," which here we define as "the human ability to adapt the cognitive processing strategies to face new and unexpected conditions in the environment" (Cañas et al. 2005, 95). Those with cognitive flexibility are better able to do the following:

- view situations from multiple perspectives
- learn and apply new information to situations
- take information and strategies from one situation and apply them to another
- brainstorm alternative solutions to problems
- deal with unexpected changes

Unsurprisingly, cognitive flexibility is just as important for troubleshooters as it is for electronic resources librarians, especially given that many access troubleshooters are e-resources librarians themselves. By making an effort to improve cognitive flexibility—through mental training, reframing exercises, and online resources—troubleshooters can increase their effectiveness, both at work and in life.

Although improving cognitive flexibility is possible, success relies solely on individuals' personal motivation and their ability to reframe their own innate ways of thinking. Team leaders can identify and nurture these beneficial traits in others, but they cannot force people to improve their own cognitive flexibility. They can only expose others to these new concepts, demonstrate the relevance of those concepts to the library's troubleshooting workflow, and hope the team members are then inspired to improve their own troubleshooting skills.

TROUBLESHOOTING INFRASTRUCTURE AND WORKFLOW

Troubleshooting infrastructure and workflow also play an important part in the effectiveness of access troubleshooting. By infrastructure, we mean the physical and organizational structures used to facilitate troubleshooting. This includes various technologies, such as help ticket systems and diagnosis tools, as well as the organization, support, and staffing provided by library leadership. The infrastructure available to troubleshooters may or may not be within their ability to modify or control; however, it can have a profound impact on the scope and effectiveness of a library's troubleshooting workflow.

For instance, consider the effect of staffing on how, where, and why troubleshooting occurs. Libraries with a robust troubleshooting staff, such as two or three full-time staff members who devote a portion of their time to troubleshooting, may be able to meet a variety of needs in a wider number of places and in a timelier manner. These staff members are likely to be more knowledgeable about the library's technology and access mechanisms and will have both the time and expertise to address systemic issues rather than simply putting out fires. However, they may also face challenges in coordinating with each other and, as a result, may adopt technologies that help them organize their efforts.

Libraries with a lean troubleshooting staff, by contrast, may have to make compromises regarding when, where, and how quickly they respond to problem reports. The focus will likely be on putting out fires rather than on proactive checks, clean-up projects, or addressing systemic issues. This, in turn, could impact the level of service experienced by the library's patrons. However, because the staff is limited as to where and when access issues are reported and addressed, they may not have a need for complicated organizational technologies and may opt for simpler workflows.

Similarly, the number of staff devoted to maintaining and addressing the e-resources life cycle will directly impact any troubleshooting efforts. First, without enough staff, there will inherently be more access issues due to changes in subscriptions, platforms, vendors, or resources that have not been recorded within the library system; and, then, with more errors present, troubleshooting staff will struggle to keep pace with the problems being reported and the amount of maintenance required to address such systemic issues. The support provided by library leadership in this area is therefore vital.

The customer service culture that adequate infrastructure promotes is important to the success of a troubleshooting workflow. If patrons are confident that they can reach out and receive timely assistance from the library, the troubleshooting workflow will become self-perpetuating. With carefully considered, proactive workflows, library troubleshooters will know what to do, experience less confusion, and transmit their satisfaction of working within a well-organized troubleshooting workflow to both patrons and their library coworkers. We discuss project management and designing effective, proactive workflows more in chapter 7.

Conclusion

Many factors influence the success of an e-resources troubleshooter. The biggest differentiator in success between a novice and an expert troubleshooter is level of technical knowledge, but troubleshooters can further increase their effectiveness by learning various troubleshooting strategies and methodologies. Internal qualities like motivation, curiosity, and cognitive flexibility also play an important role, and these can be nurtured within both the individual and the troubleshooting team. These qualities can be stymied, however, if the appropriate infrastructure and organizational support are not forthcoming. Therefore, it is important to look holistically at a library's troubleshooting process, including continued training and support, in order to foster efficiency, effectiveness, and a culture of customer service.

ADDITIONAL READINGS AND RESOURCES

Davis, Randall. 1983. "Reasoning from First Principles in Electronic Troubleshooting." *International Journal of Man-Machine Studies* 19 (5): 403–23.

Dostál, Jiří. 2015. "Theory of Problem Solving." *Procedia—Social and Behavioral Sciences* 174: 2798–805.

Emery, Jill, Graham Stone, and Peter McCracken. 2020. *Techniques for Electronic Resource Management: TERMS and the Transition to Open.* Chicago: ALA Editions.

George, Frank. 1980. *Problem Solving.* London: Duckworth.

Haan, Alexander, and Pauline de Heer. 2012. *Solving Complex Problems: Professional Group Decision-Making Support in Highly Complex Situations.* The Hague, Netherlands: Eleven International Publishing.

Harlow, Harry. 1951. "Thinking." In *Theoretical Foundations of Psychology*, edited by Harry Nelson, 452–505. New York: Van Nostrand.

Lawson, Emma, Roën Janyk, and Rachel A. Erb. 2014. "Getting to the Core of the Matter: Competencies for New E-resources Librarians." *Serials Librarian* 66 (1–4): 153–60.

Perez, Ray S. 1991. "A View from Troubleshooting." In *Toward a Unified Theory of Problem Solving: Views from the Content Domains*, edited by Mike U. Smith, 115–53. Hillsdale, NJ: Lawrence Erlbaum.

Sioukas, Tasos. 2003. *The Solution Path: A Step-by-Step Guide to Turning Your Workplace Problems into Opportunities.* San Francisco: Jossey-Bass.

Sutton, Sarah. 2011. "Identifying Core Competencies for Electronic Resources Librarians in the Twenty-First Century Library." PhD diss., Texas Woman's University. https://repositories.tdl.org/tamucc-ir/handle/1969.6/33.

REFERENCES

Cañas, Jose J., Adoración Antolí, Inmaculada Fajardo, and Ladislao Salmerón. 2005. "Cognitive Inflexibility and the Development and Use of Strategies for Solving Complex Dynamic Problems: Effects of Different Types of Training." *Theoretical Issues in Ergonomics Science* 6 (1): 95–108. doi:10.1080/14639220512331311599.

Carter, Sunshine, and Stacie Traill. 2017. "Essential Skills and Knowledge for Trouble-shooting E-resources Access Issues in a Web-Scale Discovery Environment." *Journal of Electronic Resources Librarianship* 29 (1): 1–15. doi:10.1080/19411 26X.2017.1270096.

Duncker, Karl. 1945. *On Problem-Solving.* Psychological Monographs, no. 270. Washington, DC: American Psychological Association.

Francisco, John M., and Carolyn A. Maher. 2005. "Conditions for Promoting Reasoning in Problem Solving: Insights from a Longitudinal Study." *Journal of Mathematical Behavior* 24 (3): 361–72.

Gugerty, Leo. 2007. "Cognitive Components of Troubleshooting Strategies." *Thinking and Reasoning* 13 (2): 134–63. doi:10.1080/13546780600750641.

Huber, George. 1980. *Managerial Decision Making.* Management Applications Series. Glenview, IL: Scott, Foresman.

Jonassen, David. 2010. "Troubleshooting and Diagnosis Problems." In *Learning to Solve Problems: A Handbook for Designing Problem-Solving Learning Environment*, 77–105. New York: Routledge.

Jonassen, David, and Woei Hung. 2006. "Learning to Troubleshoot: A New Theory-Based Design Architecture." *Educational Psychology Review* 18 (1): 77–114.

Lester, Frank K., and Paul K. Kehle. 2003. "From Problem Solving to Modeling: The Evolution of Thinking about Research on Complex Mathematical Activity." In *Beyond Constructivism: Models and Modeling Perspectives on Mathematics Problem Solving, Learning, and Teaching*, edited by Richard A. Lesh and Helen M. Doerr, 501–17. Mahwah, NJ: Lawrence Erlbaum.

Mayer, Richard E. 1998. "Cognitive, Metacognitive, and Motivational Aspects of Problem Solving." *Instructional Science* 26 (1): 49–63.

———. 2013. "Problem Solving." In *The Oxford Handbook of Cognitive Psychology*, edited by Daniel Reisberg, 769–78. Oxford: Oxford University Press.

NASIG (North American Serials Interest Group). 2019. "NASIG Core Competencies for Electronic Resources Librarians." www.nasig.org/Competencies-Eresources.

Pólya, George. 1945. *How to Solve It: A New Aspect of Mathematical Method.* Princeton, NJ: Princeton University Press.

Ross, Craig, and R. Robert Orr. 2009. "Teaching Structured Troubleshooting: Integrating a Standard Methodology into an Information Technology Program." *Educational Technology Research and Development* 57 (2): 251–65.

Schaafstal, Alma, Jan Maarten Schraagen, and Marcel van Berl. 2000. "Cognitive Task Analysis and Innovation of Training: The Case of Structured Troubleshooting." *Human Factors: The Journal of Human Factors and Ergonomics Society* 42 (1): 75–86.

Schoenfeld, Alan H. 1985. *Mathematical Problem Solving.* Orlando, FL: Academic Press.

Stevens, Michael, and British Institute of Management. 1988. *Practical Problem Solving for Managers.* London: Kogan Page, in association with the British Institute of Management.

2

The Access Chain

The importance of understanding your library's technical system cannot be overstated. As noted in the previous chapter, the biggest differentiator between novice and advanced troubleshooters is the depth of their technical knowledge. This makes sense, of course. The more a troubleshooter is familiar with the inner workings of the system, the better that person is at intuiting where and why things break—and, ultimately, how to fix them. With the complexity and diversity of technologies employed within a library's system, obtaining the necessary technical knowledge can be an intimidating prospect, especially to those without a tech background. However, you do not need to be a computer genius to effectively troubleshoot. By simply understanding the top-down view of your library's technical system—that is, the basic flow of access and the way the various technologies interact with each other—you, as a troubleshooter, can dramatically improve your capability.

In this chapter, we introduce you to this top-down view of a library's system. We begin by focusing on the base technical components that go into providing access, describing how each component works, the role it plays within the larger library system, and how you can use these components to develop a mental model of your library's access chains. We then walk through some commonly employed access chains while discussing the various spheres of control under which each segment of the chain falls. Finally, we end the chapter with a brief questionnaire to direct your inquiries when mapping out your own library's access chains and connect you to resources for further reading.

Terminology

Library technology is constantly in flux. Every day new ideas, products, and tools emerge onto the landscape, reshaping our thinking and blurring the lines between previously distinct concepts and terminology. This has led to the proliferation and obfuscation of library technical nomenclature and resulted in terms with similar or interchangeable meanings. As we begin our discussion of access chains, we ask for the reader to bear this fluidity in mind. While we have taken care in selecting and defining our terminology so as to best facilitate the conversation, we also acknowledge that we may not have captured all the iterations or variations currently in use. In this section, we define the terminology that will appear throughout this book.

COMPUTER TERMINOLOGY

API, or application programming interface, is a set of programming rules that enable two computer systems or applications to talk to each other. Programmers use APIs to create intermediary software that works behind the scenes, allowing one computer system to submit queries, execute commands, and retrieve data from another. Within libraries, APIs are commonly employed by discovery interfaces and web-scale discovery services to provide additional features and functionality for patrons, such as search results from third-party applications.

Authentication is the process of proving one's identity as an authorized or legitimate user of a product or service. Most vendors and content providers require that patrons first prove their affiliation with the purchasing or subscribing library before they are allowed to access content on the platform. Libraries employ various methods of authentication, including username/password, internet protocol (IP) address, proxy server, virtual private network (VPN), and single sign-on (SSO).

Caches store pieces of information about a website, such as logos, background images, JavaScript, CSS (cascading style sheets), and HTML (hypertext markup language) code. By storing this information, a browser is able to load a website more quickly if visited again.

Cookies are small pieces of information about a user's activities or preferences on a website. Like cache information, cookies are stored in a browser when visiting a website and are accessed again if the browser returns.

HTML, or hypertext markup language, is a web coding language that uses tags, denoted by the symbols < and >, to create web pages. HTML is usually paired with CSS (a stylesheet that defines the appearance of a website) and JavaScript (a programming language). We will not be covering CSS or JavaScript in this book.

Hyperlinks are clickable electronic links that lead directly from one web page or web resource to another. *Permalinks* are permanent hyperlinks.

IP (internet protocol) *addresses* represent the specific locations of computers or other electronic devices on a network. Large institutions, such as university campuses and public libraries, have *IP ranges* that represent the array of each institution's available IP addresses.

Platforms, as used in electronic resource management, are the overall web environment (i.e., website) used to host an e-resource application or service. Platforms usually correspond with specific vendors, but vendors may have multiple platforms.

Proxies are a type of intermediary server or software system that sits between one computer and another. Libraries commonly employ proxies to authenticate remotely located patrons because a proxy enables a library to override a patron computer's IP address with its own, thus changing the computer's apparent location. The most commonly employed proxy system for libraries is EZproxy.

Servers are computers that provide data or services to other computers (called *clients*) over a network like the internet. There are many types of servers, including web servers that provide access to websites.

Single sign-on (SSO) is a form of authentication that uses session information stored as a cookie on a web browser to enable third-party resources and vendors to share a person's credentials among themselves. Signing in with a Google account to a third-party service is an example of using single sign-on.

URLs, or uniform resource locators, are the web addresses of resources, such as web pages, images, files, and so forth, on a computer network like the internet. URLs begin with either http:// or https://, with the latter indicating that the website is more secure.

VPNs, or virtual private networks, are services that create a secure, encrypted connection from one computer to another. Similar to a proxy, a VPN acts as a middleman for a computer and its destination, sitting between them and overriding the connecting computer's IP address with its own. However, unlike a proxy, a VPN is more secure because it encrypts a computer's information before it even connects to the internet.

LIBRARY TECHNOLOGY TERMINOLOGY

Access tools, sometimes called discovery or retrieval tools, are any computer application through which a library user can discover and gain access to an electronic resource. Features and functionality vary greatly from tool to tool, and libraries typically employ multiple tools in order to meet a variety of access needs. Types of access tools include online catalogs (also known as OPACs or online public access catalogs), discovery interfaces, database A–Z lists, e-journal A–Z lists, research guides, and web-scale discovery services.

Central indexes are "the collection of preharvested and processed metadata and full text that comprises the searchable content of a [web-scale discovery] service" (Hoeppner 2012, 7). A central index is populated by vendor-supplied resource data, which, depending on the agreements in place with the publisher or content provider, could include resource abstracts, tables of contents, and full text, in addition to citation information. When paired with a discovery interface, a central index is able to provide article-level search results and linking to patrons.

Database A–Z lists are alphabetical lists of databases (and other selected e-resources) to which a library provides access. Libraries create these lists through a variety of methods, which range from manually adding hyperlinks to a static web page to developing a home-grown database solution to employing a vendor product, such as Springshare's LibGuides A–Z Database List. While these A–Z lists primarily consist of databases or database-like resources, librarians often choose to include other types of e-resources or web tools that they believe will prove helpful to patrons. The more advanced A–Z lists may also include options to search or browse by subject, topic, or tag and often display additional information about the resource, such as a brief description or notes concerning access, use, or authentication.

Direct linking is an alternative to OpenURL linking and is "often implemented in discovery services to provide more reliable access to electronic resources than through the OpenURL process, making use of internal or proprietary data beyond what would be available through OpenURL" (Breeding 2018, 7).

Discovery interfaces are public-facing search applications patrons use to discover and gain access to library resources. Unlike a traditional online catalog, which is limited to searching the catalog's bibliographic contents, discovery interfaces are able to ingest and index content from a variety of sources, including institutional repositories, digital collections, and APIs (Breeding 2018). Furthermore, they provide users with advanced search and discovery features, such as keyword recommenders, limiters, facets, and relevancy ranking of results. These features are meant to encourage more serendipitous discovery rather than strict known-item retrieval.

Discovery services, sometimes called index-based discovery services or web-scale discovery services, are products that combine a discovery interface with a central index. Unlike a stand-alone discovery interface, which is not connected to a central index, a discovery service is able to facilitate the discovery of resources outside of a library's holdings via its connection to its central index. Other advanced features include article-level search results and linking.

E-journal A–Z lists, like their database counterparts, are simply alphabetical lists of electronic journals to which a library provides access. However, unlike a database A–Z list, which is composed of individually crafted entries, these lists are typically autopopulated in accordance with the library's holdings. Besides acting as a searchable inventory of a library's e-journals, an A–Z list also collates and displays each e-journal's available access points as well as other relevant information, such as coverage dates and notes regarding licensing and authentication.

ERMS, or electronic resource management system, is a knowledge management system that specializes in tracking and managing electronic resources throughout their life cycle. An ERMS is typically powered by a centralized knowledge base that allows librarians to easily find and activate specific instances of e-resources or e-packages and includes additional management features, such as the ability to store payment, licensing, and contact information; to receive renewal reminders; and to track usage.

ILS, or integrated library system, is a suite of modules used by librarians to manage the activities involved in acquiring and loaning materials, such as ordering, invoicing, cataloging, and circulation. ILSs were originally developed to provide operational support for physical materials and as a result are poorly equipped to handle the complexities of e-resource management. These inadequacies have prompted the development of other tools, such as ERMSs, A–Z lists, and LSPs (library services platforms).

Knowledge bases are centralized databases of metadata that describe specific instances of e-resources available through a publisher, content provider, or platform (Wilson 2016). A knowledge base includes not just basic bibliographic information (title, author, publisher, etc.) but also information about the resource's platform, vendor, coverage dates, and access model, including which packages or collections it appears in. Knowledge bases are used to power a variety of knowledge management systems and access tools. The primary purpose of the knowledge base is holdings management, allowing libraries to track which e-resources they have with certain vendors. This, in turn, supports the article-level links patrons encounter in a library's discovery service and the title-level links in a library's A–Z lists (Talbott and Zmau 2018).

Knowledge management system refers to any computer system that libraries use to keep themselves organized and to make resources discoverable to their patrons. Many types of knowledge management systems have sprung up over the years, but they are usually centered around recording and managing particular elements of library resources, such as bibliographic, holdings, vendor, or access information. It is important to understand what knowledge management system(s) your library employs, who is responsible for maintaining it, and what sort of information it contains. Examples include ERMSs, ILSs, LSPs, and link resolver services.

Link resolver refers to the "specialized software used to provide context-sensitive links among the panoply of systems that compose a modern library's electronic collections" (Chisare et al. 2017, 93). Utilizing the OpenURL encoding format, link resolvers create their links by combining the citation data of the desired resource (source) from a library discovery record with the provider website (target) linking parameters necessary to connect to the desired resource. For a link resolver to know which resources are locally available to a library patron, it must be connected to a knowledge base that has been prepopulated with a library's electronic holdings. See figure 2.1.

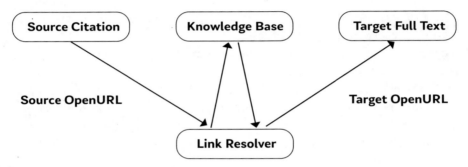

Source Citation:
Kasprowski, Rafal. "NISO's IOTA Initiative: Measuring the Quality of OpenURL Links." *The Serials Librarian* 62, no. 1–4 (2012): 95–102.

Target OpenURL:
https://institution-in.userservices.exlibrisgroup.com/view/uresolver/01_INST/openurl?rft.atitle=
**NISO's%20IOTA%20Initiative:%20Measuring%20the%20Quality%20of%20OpenURL%20
Links**&rft.jtitle=**The%20Serials%20Librarian**&rft.au=**Kasprowski%20Rafal**&rft.date=**2012**&rft
.volume=**62**&rft.issue=**1-4**&rft.spage=**95**&rft.epage=**102**&rft.pages=**95-102**&rft.issn=**0361-526X**&rft
.eissn=**1541-1095**

FIGURE 2.1
OpenURL link resolver syntax diagram

LSP, or library services platform, refers to next-generation library systems that incorporate the functionalities of an ILS, knowledge base, link resolver, and ERMS. LSPs were developed as a way to unite the disparate knowledge management systems into one comprehensive system and support the workflows of electronic, digital, and physical material.

MARC records, or machine-readable cataloging records, are a type of computer file that contains bibliographic information about a library resource. This includes standard bibliographic metadata, such as title, author, publication information, and subject headings, in addition to access information, such as call numbers for physical materials and URLs for electronic resources. Although MARC records have evolved greatly since their original development in the 1960s, they are still primarily geared toward describing physical, rather than electronic, materials. As a result, MARC records have some shortcomings and hurdles when it comes to accurately representing e-resources, particularly regarding the complexities of provider, platform, e-package, and article-level information.

Online catalogs, also known as OPACs, or online public access catalogs, are electronic databases composed of bibliographic MARC records. An online catalog acts as an inventory of the library's available resources, with patrons able to find and retrieve resource information through its simplistic, Boolean-based search interface. To keep the catalog's inventory up-to-date, librarians must continually add, remove, or modify MARC records to reflect changes in library holdings or resource information. Because of their reliance on MARC records, online catalogs are poorly equipped to handle electronic resources, which are complex and constantly in flux. Other tools have sprung up to address these shortcomings, but many libraries continue to load MARC records into their catalogs for certain types of electronic resources. The practice of each library will vary; however, some load MARC records into their catalogs for such items as individually purchased or subscribed e-books and e-journals, titles within certain e-book and e-journal packages, patron-driven acquisition or demand-driven acquisition (PDA/DDA) titles, and databases or aggregators.

Research guides are curated collections of information resources, including physical, electronic, and web-based materials, that a librarian has recommended for a particular subject, topic, or academic course. Generally taking the form of a web page, a research guide combines a resource's access information, such as its call number or URL, with advice and explanations about its use (Talbott and Zmau 2018). Research guides are a popular access tool among subject specialists and liaisons, who create them as finding aids for patrons in order to highlight resources that might otherwise be overlooked or difficult to access.

Mental Models

Researchers in the field of cognitive psychology have long known the important role mental models play in effective troubleshooting. Beyond just technical know-how, a mental model is an "understanding of a system that includes knowledge of the possible states of each component as well as temporal and causal links between components" (Kurland and Tenney 1988, 60). Troubleshooters who develop a strong mental model of a system are able to visualize not only what each component is and does but also how those components interact and effect changes within each other. When practically applied, a mental model can "serve as a tool for problem solving by allowing the thinker to mentally 'run' the model to observe the effects that a change in one part of the system has on other parts" (Kurland and Tenney 1988, 60).

Although a troubleshooter's mental model will naturally mature as the troubleshooter gains experience, that growth can be stymied in complex environments, particularly where responsibility for various components is distributed among separate departments and staff. Given the complicated nature of library systems, which rely on multiple technologies, vendors, and library departments working seamlessly together, developing a well-rounded mental model can be overwhelming. To help foster the development of your mental model, we have chosen to illustrate the various components of access and their interactions in what we are calling *access chains*, or the paths of interconnected technologies a patron travels through in order to gain access to an e-resource.

Components of Access: Authentication and Common Access Chains

Library systems are composed of four general types of components: access tools, knowledge management systems, linking systems, and authentication. Regardless of how your library chooses to configure its technology or which vendor or vendors it employs, these four pieces must be present to grant a patron access. This basic access chain is depicted in figure 2.2.

The flow of access is as follows:

1. From a computer, smartphone, or other personal device, a patron navigates to an access tool using a browser.
2. The access tool, which is populated by some type of knowledge management system, whether that be a CMS (content management system), an ILS, an ERMS, or an LSP, or some combination thereof, presents the patron with options for discovering the record of a resource.
3. Once a patron locates the record of a desired resource within the access tool, the patron clicks on the accompanying link.

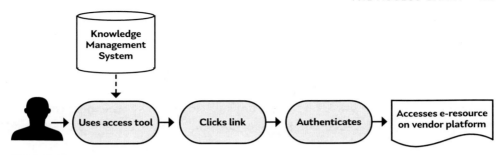

FIGURE 2.2
The basic access chain

4. The link then connects to the resource, either directly or through a link-resolving process, like OpenURL.
5. Assuming the resource is not freely available, a patron will then be confronted with a request to prove affiliation with the library through an authentication process.
6. If successful in authenticating, the patron is then allowed access to the e-resource on the vendor's platform.

A similar flow happens with each of a library's available access tools. However, many libraries employ multiple access tools, knowledge management systems, and authentication methods, which increases the complexity and interconnectedness as the chains begin to overlap. The complexity is further compounded by the varying degrees that each component in the chain is controlled and maintained by the patron, library, or vendor. This is particularly true regarding the metadata utilized in the access tools and knowledge management systems, which often blends library-controlled metadata alongside metadata created and maintained by the vendor.

To get a handle on this complexity, we have found it helpful to think through the various access chains in isolation, highlighting under whose control each piece of the chain falls, and then to build your library's full access chain by combining the pieces together. In this section, we outline several access chains that are commonly employed by libraries. Throughout each chain, as represented in the figures, we also demarcate the spheres of control (patron, library, vendor) under which each component falls:

- black = patron-controlled metadata, system, or tool
- gray = library-controlled metadata, system, or tool
- white = vendor-controlled metadata, system, or tool

AUTHENTICATION

In the basic access chain depicted in figure 2.2, the authentication process occurs once the patron has clicked on a link in a resource record, but before the patron is able to access the e-resource on the vendor's platform. This is the most common place for authentication to occur; however, it is not the only place it can. Depending on the e-resource, the patron's physical location, and the method of authentication, a patron may authenticate earlier, later, or not at all. In our subsequent access chains, we have chosen to illustrate only one authentication method—proxy—in order to avoid cluttering the diagrams. However, before we proceed to our first access chain, we want to take a closer look at the possible authentication methods and how the placement of authentication within the access chain would vary depending on which method is employed.

Authentication via IP Address

IP address authentication is one of the most popular ways to authenticate library patrons. It works like this: when a library acquires an e-resource, it provides the vendor with a set of IP ranges that represents the library's computer and Wi-Fi network. When a patron connects to the e-resource over the internet, the vendor checks the device's IP address to see if it falls within the previously provided IP ranges. If it does, the patron is granted access. If not, the patron is redirected to an error or a payment message. Because this process happens behind the scenes, the patron is never prompted to enter credentials, making the movement from discovery record to e-resource appear seamless.

Unfortunately, IP address authentication by itself is able to provide access only for patrons who are currently located on the library's or institution's physical campus. Once the patron wanders outside the institution's Wi-Fi range, the patron loses access. As a result, IP address authentication is frequently used in conjunction with other authentication methods in order to grant access to patrons who are located remotely.

Authentication via Proxy Server

In order to provide access to remote patrons, many libraries use a proxy server, or proxy, jointly with IP address authentication (see figure 2.3). As you will recall from the earlier terminology section, a proxy is a type of intermediary server or software system that sits between one computer and another. When a remotely located patron attempts to connect to an e-resource through one of the library's access tools, the browser is redirected to the proxy server, which asks for the patron's credentials—typically, username and password. The browser redirect can happen a couple different ways but typically involves modifying the e-resource's URL, such as by adding a proxy prefix to the beginning of the

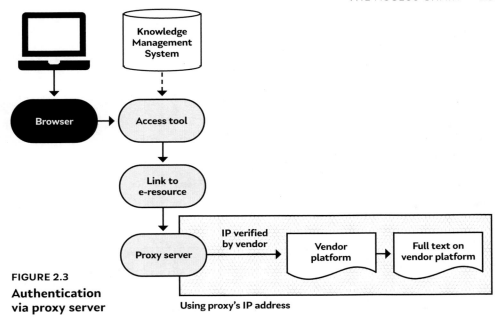

FIGURE 2.3
**Authentication
via proxy server**

e-resource's URL. This is an example proxy prefix: https://proxy.yourlibrary.org/login?url=. Once the proxy verifies the patron's credentials against its internal database, it connects the browser to the desired resource using its own IP address. Because the proxy server's IP address is included in the authorized IP ranges given to vendors, the patron is granted access to the e-resource.

In addition to the proxy prefix, a proxy requires maintenance of several configuration files in order to function, including one that contains the URLs, hosts, and domains of the library's e-resources licensed for IP address authentication and access. The configuration file needs to be frequently updated to keep pace with vendor platform developments, and an outdated configuration file can often be the source of access issues.

Authentication for the patron technically happens twice with this method: once when the patron's credentials are verified by the proxy server and once again when the proxy's IP address is verified by the vendor platform. This means the responsibility for configuration and maintenance is split between the proxy service provider and the vendor. Depending on which issues arise, one or both may need to be contacted in order to enact a solution. Also, if the proxy server is hosted locally, rather than with a consortium or third-party provider, maintenance responsibility may be split among several staff members or departments.

Authentication via VPN
Another way to provide access to remote patrons is through a virtual private network. A VPN fills a role similar to that of a proxy, acting as an intermediary between the patron's device and the desired e-resource. Just like with a proxy,

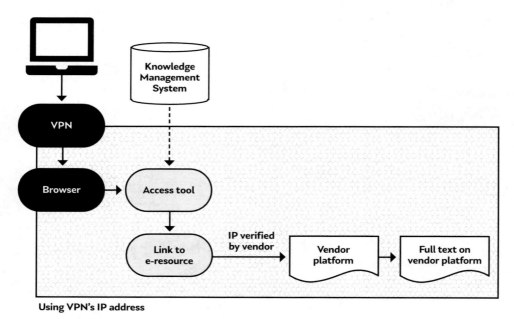

FIGURE 2.4
Authentication via VPN

a patron's device must first connect to the VPN, thus assuming its IP, before connecting to the e-resource. Because the VPN's IP address is included in the IP ranges provided to the vendor, the device appears to be located "on campus" and is authorized for access.

However, unlike a proxy, a VPN does not use website redirects or URL modification. Instead, patrons download and install specialized software onto their personal devices, configuring it with settings specific to their institution. Whenever patrons want to use the VPN, they launch the program and authenticate with their username and password—all before opening a browser or navigating to an access tool. Because the log-in happens within the software on the patron's device, rather than in a browser, authentication occurs in two places: at the beginning of the access chain, when the VPN verifies the patron's credentials, and again toward the end, when the vendor verifies the VPN's IP address. Responsibility for assisting patrons with the VPN varies but is usually handled by an institution's IT department.

It is important to note that not all institutions' VPN services are configured to provide access to e-resources. Some institutions implement a practice called split tunneling, which means the VPN routes only certain types of web traffic through its server, while the rest access the internet normally. Institutions that use split tunneling generally route only traffic destined for internal resources, such as those hosted on an institution's intranet, through the VPN; all other traffic, including that going to library e-resources, accesses the internet using the patron's normal router and IP address. This means if the patron is off campus, he or she will not be authenticated correctly. Before suggesting a patron use a VPN service for authentication, you will want to ensure that it does not use split tunneling.

Authentication via Single Sign-On

Single sign-on (SSO) is unique among authentication methods because it relies on storing session information as a cookie on a patron's browser rather than on manipulating IP addresses. With SSO, a patron can navigate to an e-resource from anywhere on the internet, including Google, and be able to log in by choosing his or her institution from the provided dropdown menu, often called a WAYF (Where Are You From?), on the vendor's platform. Once a patron logs in, the information (called a token) is stored as a cookie on the browser, which can then be shared by other resources and vendors without the patron needing to log in again. Because SSO requires vendors to install and configure additional software on their servers, not every vendor will have SSO as an option. As a result, SSO is often used in conjunction with other authentication methods, such as a proxy server, in order to provide robust coverage.

Authentication via Vendor Platform Username/Password

If a vendor does not support any of the authentication methods just discussed, then it likely supports username/password (U/P) authentication. The U/P credentials used for authentication are not the same as those issued to patrons by the library or institution. Instead, they are unique to the vendor platform and are either provided by the vendor to the subscribing library (who then disseminates them to patrons) or generated for individual patrons upon registering with the vendor, whether done by the patrons themselves or by a librarian. In both cases, authentication happens by entering the U/P on the vendor's platform.

Now that we have covered authentication within the basic access chain, we move forward with our discussion of the other components of access. We then combine these individual portions into the most common library system setups.

RESEARCH GUIDE ACCESS CHAIN

Let's begin by looking at one of the simpler access chains. Figure 2.5 depicts an example of how a patron could gain access to an e-resource via a subject-specific research guide. Here, the patron begins at the library website and navigates to the research guide, selecting a link on the guide page and authenticating via a proxy before being taken to the e-resource content on the vendor's platform. Within this chain, patrons have control over which device, browser, and browser settings they use to navigate the chain and access the e-resource. They also control what credentials they enter to be authenticated via the proxy. If an issue originates with any of these pieces—device, browser and browser settings, or the entered authentication credentials—it is the patron who must make modifications to resolve the issue.

The library is responsible for maintaining its website and the research guide, which includes populating the guide with accurate and properly constructed links. Because the links within the research guides are usually manually entered by librarians, rather than autopopulated, the links are prone to errors. If an incorrect link is provided to patrons, it is up to library staff to fix it. The library is also responsible for maintaining the proxy server, particularly the configuration file, which is used to authenticate patrons.

Finally, the vendor is responsible for maintaining its own platform, including ensuring its advertised features, functionality, and (most important) contents are accessible to authorized users. Vendors who prioritize customer service employ proactive workflows to prevent platform and content issues. However, even

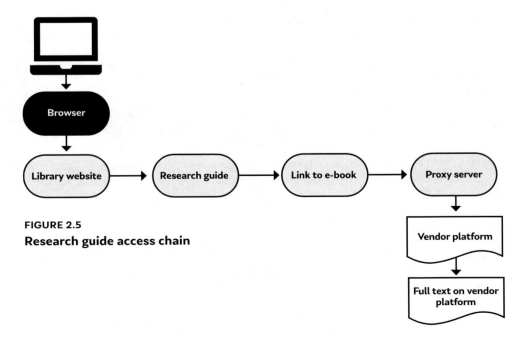

FIGURE 2.5
Research guide access chain

with the best intentions, issues still occur. When an issue arises, it is ultimately the library's responsibility to notify the vendor about the issue and, in turn, the vendor's responsibility to implement a fix.

DISCOVERY INTERFACE ACCESS CHAIN

Figure 2.6 depicts a potential access chain featuring a discovery interface. Unlike the research guide in the previous chain, a discovery interface is populated by multiple data sources, including "catalog records, digital library items, institutional repository holdings, institutional bibliography materials, and other library collections and resources" (Berenstein and Katz 2012). Most of these data sources are managed at the local library level, and it is the library's responsibility to maintain and update them. Article-level results can also be populated within the discovery interface if the library has an agreement in place with an outside service to bring in the data via API. Discovery interfaces with this functionality include Innovative Interfaces' Encore Duet and SirsiDynix's Enterprise. Any corrections or maintenance of article-level results would be the responsibility of vendors.

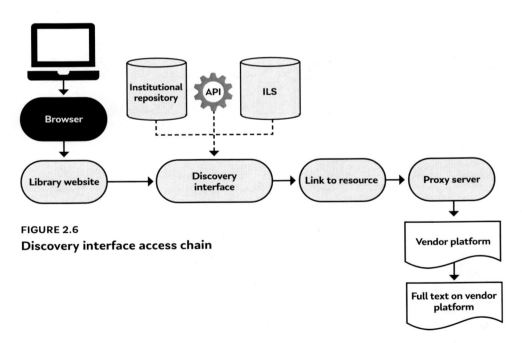

FIGURE 2.6
Discovery interface access chain

KNOWLEDGE BASE ACCESS CHAIN

Knowledge bases are a central fixture in the remainder of our access chains. As you will recall from our earlier definitions list, a knowledge base is a centralized database consisting of both bibliographic metadata and information about the resource's platform, vendor, available dates, and access model. This information is curated from publishers, aggregators, and content providers by the knowledge base vendor and provided to libraries as a way to track their e-resource holdings.

In figure 2.7, we depict how a knowledge base is utilized within an electronic resource management system (ERMS) to populate holdings in an e-journal A–Z list. Because the ERMS's knowledge base is a vendor-managed product populated by information supplied by various providers, the vendor is responsible for maintaining its accuracy and timeliness. However, librarians are responsible for using the administrative features of the ERMS to correctly select the resources and local holdings information that apply to their specific institutions. If a librarian selects an incorrect journal or coverage range from the knowledge base, it is up to the librarian, not the vendor, to fix the error. It is from this combination of vendor-supplied and librarian-selected information that the e-journal A–Z list is generated.

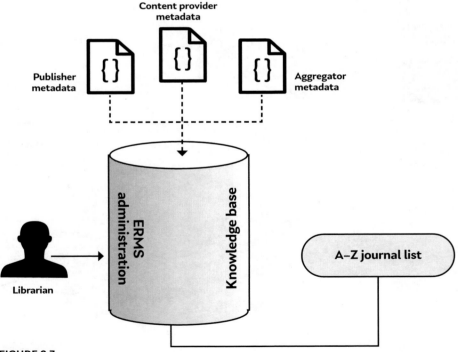

FIGURE 2.7
Knowledge base access chain

DISCOVERY SERVICE ACCESS CHAIN

A discovery service is populated by data from many sources. In figure 2.8, we have depicted some of the common sources of data, including records from an ILS, institutional repository, API, and ERMS/knowledge base (KB in the figure). Although the library has direct control over the records that are created and published within both an ILS and an institutional repository, responsibility for maintaining correct records within the ERMS is split between the librarians, who track holdings, and the vendor, who controls the underlying metadata present within the knowledge base.

In addition to these title-level records, a discovery service is also populated by a central index that provides discovery for various pieces comprising those titles, such as articles, book chapters, abstracts, images, videos, and tables of contents. Through the metadata furnished by a central index, a discovery service is able to provide article-level search results and linking to patrons, which is the primary difference between it and a discovery interface. While librarians may be able to effect some change over the amount of information supplied from the central index to the discovery service, responsibility for timely and accurate metadata within the index itself lies solely with the discovery service vendor.

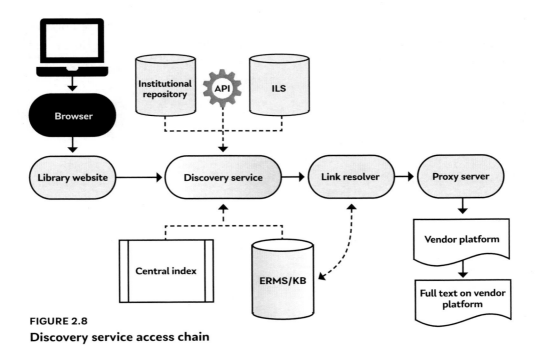

FIGURE 2.8
Discovery service access chain

COMPREHENSIVE ACCESS CHAIN

In figure 2.9, we have combined all of the access chains introduced thus far into a single comprehensive access chain that is meant to represent one possible configuration of pathways for a library's patrons to gain access to an e-resource. The diagram details some of the most common access tools, knowledge management systems, linking options, authentication methods, and the various interactions between components. Of particular note: both the discovery service and the catalog interface are populated by ILS metadata; however, the discovery service has additional metadata sources, including a central index, APIs, an ERMS/knowledge base, and an institutional repository. Also, the research guide home page, database A–Z list, and e-journal A–Z list, while interconnected to various knowledge management systems, remain as stand-alone access tools as well.

We have also included an example of how patrons can begin their discovery journey outside of the library website with Google Scholar, which can be configured to utilize the library's link resolver to allow patrons to connect to the library's holdings. Other abstract and indexing (A&I) resources offer similar functionality, but it is up to the library to decide which platforms they would like it enabled on. You may wish to inventory the resources on which this functionality has been enabled to assist with troubleshooting in the future.

Another example of a comprehensive access chain comes from Sunshine Carter and Stacie Traill (2019), who diagrammed the flow of access within the primary access tools for the University of Minnesota (see figure 2.10). The layout differs slightly from the chains we previously discussed but clearly defines the library's available access tools, knowledge management systems, linking options, and authentication methods.

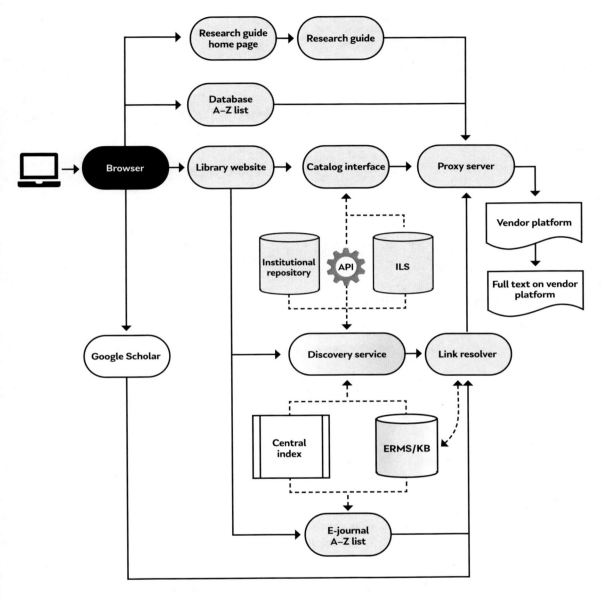

FIGURE 2.9
Comprehensive access chain

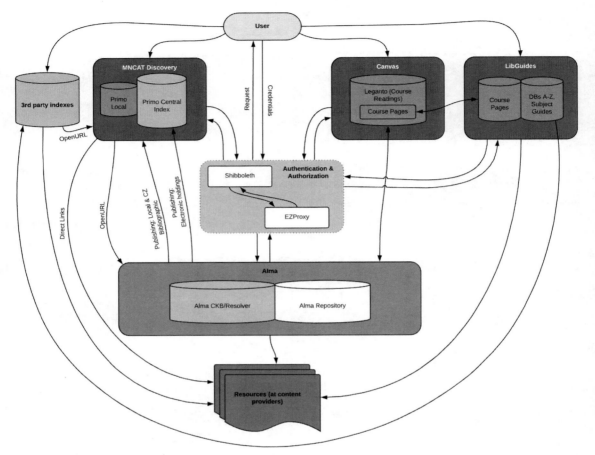

FIGURE 2.10
University of Minnesota system context diagram

Source: Carter, Sunshine, and Stacie Traill. 2019. University of Minnesota Discovery System Context Diagram. In "Teach Your Staff to Troubleshoot E-resources: Practical Processes to Documenting and Implementing a Troubleshooting Training Curriculum." Workshop presented at Electronic Resources and Libraries, Austin, TX, March 6, 2019. https://z.umn.edu/erl19ws.

LIBRARY SERVICES PLATFORM: ALMA ACCESS CHAIN

In the access chains we have discussed thus far, each of the components was developed in relative isolation from the others, requiring various publishing and integration processes to allow them to interact and function together. We next discuss library services platforms, or LSPs, that were developed to unite the disparate access chains into one inclusive system. In order to facilitate this discussion, we have chosen to focus on the Alma/Primo LSP, which integrates the functionality of an ILS, an ERMS, an institutional repository, an e-journal A–Z list, and a discovery service into one unified system, as depicted in figure 2.11.

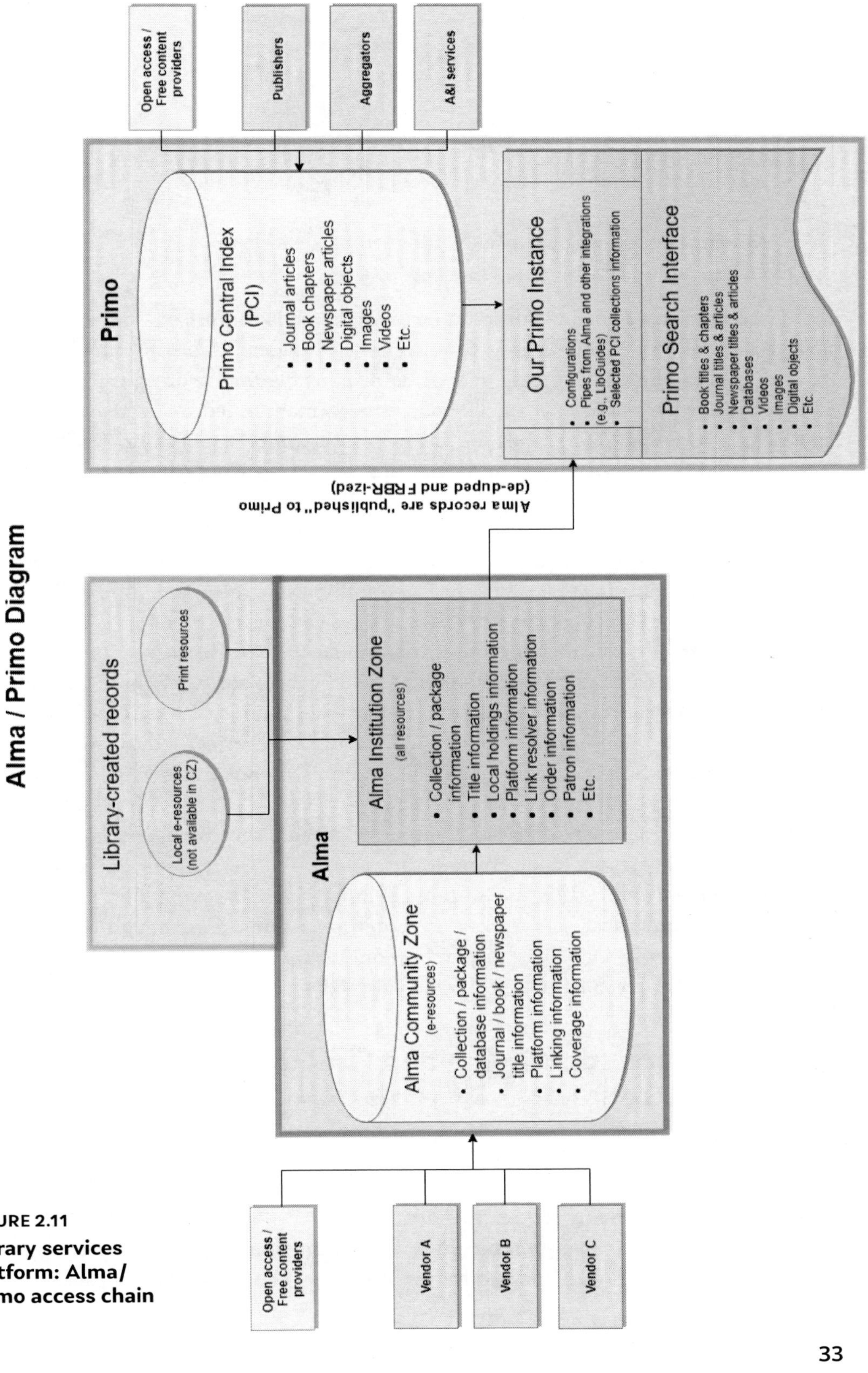

Alma / Primo Diagram

Primo

Primo Central Index (PCI)

- Journal articles
- Book chapters
- Newspaper articles
- Digital objects
- Images
- Videos
- Etc.

Open access / Free content providers

Publishers

Aggregators

A&I services

Our Primo Instance

- Configurations
- Pipes from Alma and other integrations (e.g., LibGuides)
- Selected PCI collections information

Primo Search Interface

- Book titles & chapters
- Journal titles & articles
- Newspaper titles & articles
- Databases
- Videos
- Images
- Digital objects
- Etc.

Alma records are "published" to Primo (de-duped and FRBR-ized)

Alma

Library-created records

Print resources

Local e-resources (not available in CZ)

Alma Institution Zone (all resources)

- Collection / package information
- Title information
- Local holdings information
- Platform information
- Link resolver information
- Order information
- Patron information
- Etc.

Alma Community Zone (e-resources)

- Collection / package / database information
- Journal / book / newspaper title information
- Platform information
- Linking information
- Coverage information

Open access / Free content providers

Vendor A

Vendor B

Vendor C

FIGURE 2.11
Library services platform: Alma/ Primo access chain

33

The terminology used within the Alma/Primo system differs from other library systems, so we briefly define the relevant terms here:

- Community Zone—Alma's knowledge base
- Institution Zone—the library's local holdings, including both print and electronic resources
- Network Zone—shared local holdings for a consortium
- PCI—Primo's central index

The Community Zone, like other knowledge bases, is comprised of metadata contributed by publishers, aggregators, content providers, and other libraries. Ex Libris, as the knowledge base vendor, is responsible for ensuring the metadata being ingested is promptly processed, properly maintained, and consistently made available to customers. The Institution Zone is comprised of a library's local holdings records for both print and electronic resources. These records can be loaded by librarians individually or by bulk (as is done within an ILS), or they can be localized (i.e., tracked or activated) from the Community Zone. All of these records are within the immediate control of librarians if updates are necessary; however, if the localized versions of the Community Zone records require updating, it is best practice to report the error to the vendor so the update can be disseminated to everyone using that record. Similar to the Institution Zone, the Network Zone consists of the local holdings held by a consortium. These can be either imported by librarians or localized from the Community Zone. These holdings are shared throughout the consortium by member libraries, and the responsibility of maintaining the holdings will depend on the consortium's policy and membership structure.

PCI is the central index of Primo, the LSP's discovery service. Like other central indexes, it ingests metadata from a variety of publishers, aggregators, and content providers and is thus able to provide linking and discoverability to articles, book chapters, abstracts, tables of contents, and more. Although certain customizations are available for displaying content in Primo, the responsibility of maintaining the central index rests solely with the vendor, Ex Libris.

Questionnaire: Identifying and Finding Out More about Your Local Systems

Now that we have walked through several examples of library access chains, it is time for you to start building a mental model of your own. We recommend taking time to meet with your coworkers to learn more about your local systems, who is responsible for their maintenance, and with whom you may need to work to address issues in the future. As we discuss throughout the book, resolving access issues frequently requires coordination with multiple coworkers, departments, and third-party vendors, so it is helpful to identify these points of contact ahead of time. We provide here a brief questionnaire to help guide your inquiries. We hope you use it as a jumping-off point for mapping your library's systems.

QUESTIONNAIRE

1. What methods of authentication does your library employ? (Examples include IP address, proxy server, VPN, and single sign-on.)
2. Do any of your resources fall outside the usual methods of authentication, such as requiring individual usernames/passwords?
3. Who within your organization is responsible for managing these authentication methods?
4. What access tools are employed by your library? (Examples include research guides, database A–Z list, e-journal A–Z list, discovery interface, discovery service, etc.)
5. What knowledge management system powers each of these access tools?
6. For the knowledge management systems that are under your library's control, whom within your organization would you contact for assistance with issues?
7. For the knowledge management systems that are under your vendor's control, whom within the vendor's organization would you contact for assistance with issues?
8. Does your library employ any APIs? If so, who manages them?
9. Is your link resolver enabled on any abstracting and indexing resources, such as Google Scholar, Web of Science, or PubMed?

ADDITIONAL READINGS AND RESOURCES

Botyriute, Kristina. 2018. *Access to Online Resources: A Guide for the Modern Librarian*. Cham, Switzerland: SpringerOpen.

Carter, Sunshine, and Stacie Traill. 2017. "Essential Skills and Knowledge for Troubleshooting E-resources Access Issues in a Web-Scale Discovery Environment." *Journal of Electronic Resources Librarianship* 29 (1): 1–15. doi:10.1080/19411 26X.2017.1270096.

Carter, Sunshine, and Stacie Traill. 2018. "Troubleshooting Fundamentals: A Beginner's Guide." *Online Searcher* 42 (4): 10–13.

Deodato, Joseph. 2015. "Evaluating Web-Scale Discovery: A Step-by-Step Guide." *Information Technology and Libraries* 34 (2): 19–75.

Glasser, Sarah. 2012. "Broken Links and Failed Access." *Library Resources and Technical Services* 56 (1): 14–23.

Hart, Katherine A., and Tammy S. Sugarman. 2016. "Developing an Interdepartmental Training Program for E-resources Troubleshooting." *Serials Librarian* 71 (1): 25–38. doi:10.1080/0361526X.2016.1169569.

Kasprowski, Rafal. 2012. "NISO's IOTA Initiative: Measuring the Quality of OpenURL Links." *Serials Librarian* 62 (1–4): 95–102. doi:10.1080/0361526X.2012.652480.

Koury, Regina, and Charissa Brammer. 2017. "Managing Content in EBSCO Discovery Service: Action Guide for Surviving and Thriving." *Serials Librarian* 72 (1–4): 83–86. doi:10.1080/0361526X.2017.1309828.

Kumar, Vinit. 2018. "Selecting an Appropriate Web-Scale Discovery Service: A Study of the Big 4's." *DESIDOC Journal of Library and Information Technology* 38 (6): 396–402. doi:10.14429/djlit.38.6.12860.

Landesman, Betty. 2016. "Taming the E-chaos through Standards and Best Practices: An Update on Recent Developments." *Serials Review* 42 (3): 210–15. doi:10.1080/00987 913.2016.1211443.

Pesch, Oliver. 2012. "Improving OpenURL Linking." *Serials Librarian* 63 (2): 135–45. doi:10.1080/0361526X.2012.689465.

Rosenfeld, Jenny, and Todd Enoch. 2019. "Beyond 'Set It and Forget It': Proactively Managing Your EZproxy Server." *Serials Librarian* 76 (1–4): 30–34. doi:10.1080/0361 526X.2019.1551041.

Stuart, Kenyon, Ken Varnum, and Judith Ahronheim. 2015. "Measuring Journal Linking Success from a Discovery Service." *Information Technology and Libraries* 34 (1): 52–76. doi:10.6017/ital.v34i1.5607.

van Ballegooie, Marlene, and Juliya Borie. 2015. "Facing Our E-demons: The Challenges of E-serial Management in a Large Academic Library." *Serials Librarian* 68 (1–4): 342–52. doi:10.1080/0361526X.2015.1017714.

Vaughan, Jason. 2011. "Chapter 1: Web Scale Discovery What and Why?" *Library Technology Reports* 47 (1): 5–11.

REFERENCES

Berenstein, Max, and Demian Katz. 2012. "Content Integration." *Computers in Libraries* 32 (2): 18–21.

Breeding, Marshall. 2018. "Index-Based Discovery Services: Current Market Positions and Trends." *Library Technology Reports* 54 (8): 1–33.

Carter, Sunshine, and Stacie Traill. 2019. University of Minnesota Discovery System Context Diagram. In "Teach Your Staff to Troubleshoot E-resources: Practical Processes to Documenting and Implementing a Troubleshooting Training Curriculum." Workshop presented at Electronic Resources and Libraries, Austin, TX, March 6, 2019. https://z.umn.edu/erl19ws.

Chisare, Cyndy, Jody Condit Fagan, David Gaines, and Michael Trocchia. 2017. "Selecting Link Resolver and Knowledge Base Software: Implications of Interoperability." *Journal of Electronic Resources Librarianship* 29 (2): 93–106.

Hoeppner, Athena. 2012. "The Ins and Outs of Evaluating Web-Scale Discovery Services." *Computers in Libraries* 32 (3): 6–40.

Kurland, Laura C., and Yvette J. Tenney. 1988. "The Development of Troubleshooting Expertise in Radar Mechanics." In *Intelligent Tutoring Systems: Lessons Learned*, edited by L. Dan Massey, Sharon A. Mutter, and Joseph Psotka, 59–82. Hillsdale, NJ: Lawrence Erlbaum.

Talbott, Holly, and Ashley Zmau. 2018. *Electronic Resources Librarianship: A Practical Guide for Librarians*. Lanham, MD: Rowman & Littlefield.

Wilson, Kristen. 2016. "The Knowledge Base at the Center of the Universe." *Library Technology Reports* 52 (6): 1–35.

3

Soliciting Problem Reports

In chapter 1, we discussed the seven stages that compose library trouble-shooting methodology:

1. Identify and define the problem.
2. Examine the situation.
3. Consider the possible causes.
4. Consider the possible solutions.
5. Implement the solution.
6. Review the results.
7. Communicate and document the resolution.

In this chapter, we focus on the first two steps of this methodology: identifying and defining the problem and examining the situation. We discuss the ways library access issues are uncovered and reported—and by whom—as well as the techniques for effectively gathering the information necessary to understand both the patron-focused and the technology-focused problem. We also provide example scripts and scenarios, which librarians can use and expand upon when developing their own troubleshooting workflows, and end with a discussion of user error.

Problem Reports and Problem Reporters

The first step to troubleshooting an access issue is to realize an access issue exists. Although some libraries do devote time and resources to uncovering issues through proactive checks and assessments, the number of e-resources available from a single library, which can be in the millions, generally prevents a library from continuously monitoring the accessibility of every article, book, database, and video. Instead, libraries must rely on their patrons and staff to report access issues as they are encountered, harnessing their users' collective reporting power to uncover both singular and systemic issues. Effectively soliciting and resolving problem reports, therefore, is not only good customer service, engendering trust and goodwill with patrons, but also essential for the overall health of a library's technical systems.

What do we mean by a problem report? When we refer to a problem report, we are talking about any message received by the library that indicates an access issue exists. These messages can be received through a number of submission methods but are most typically received via e-mail, online chat, online forms, phone calls, or face-to-face conversations. The messages can be submitted by a variety of reporters, including those who are internal to the library, such as circulation, resource sharing, and reference staff, and those who are external, such as students, faculty, community members, and walk-in patrons. They also can be submitted by internal reporters on behalf of external constituents, with the internal reporter sometimes performing an initial investigation or some troubleshooting legwork before passing the issue along to the troubleshooter.

Problem reports do more than just alert the library that an access issue exists; they also provide an initial definition of what problem or problems the troubleshooter will need to solve. You will recall from chapter 1 the idea of patron-focused and technology-focused problems. Patron-focused problems concern obstacles encountered by patrons when trying to fill their information needs. These obstacles could be technological or educational in nature but are always resolved once the patron's information need is filled. Technology-focused problems, conversely, concern a malfunction within the technical components of an access chain, including those controlled by the patron, library, and vendor. The problem is the result of the components not behaving as desired and is resolved only when that desired functionality is achieved. A problem report may consist of a patron-focused problem, a technology-focused problem, or both, and without enough contextual information about how, when, and where the access issue occurred, troubleshooters will not know which problems they are trying to solve.

Contextual information is also essential for conceptualizing the access issue within a troubleshooter's mind. As Mike U. Smith (1991) explains, conceptualization "involves the representation of the problem in terms that the solver understands . . . and that extract the most important components of the problem in such a way as to contribute to the ease of selection and implementation of subsequent steps" (12). For access issues, troubleshooters need more than a simple description of the obstacle or malfunction in order to fully conceptualize it; they also need to place the issue within its larger technical and temporal context. This includes knowing what access chain the reporter followed as well as when and what components feed into or interact with that chain.

For example, let's imagine that a troubleshooter received a report of a broken link to a popular market research database. Depending on where that broken link was encountered, a troubleshooter will understand and act on the issue very differently. If the broken link was located within the library's database A–Z list, for instance, the troubleshooter will know that the issue is likely affecting more people than just the reporter. This increases the urgency to find a resolution. The cause of the issue can also be restricted to just those components that compose the A–Z list access chain, such as the patron's computer setup, the A–Z list itself, and the database's platform. Components outside of this chain, such as a knowledge base or central index, do not need to be considered. In contrast, if the broken link was encountered in a discovery service, a knowledge base or central index could be vital components in understanding the issue's underlying cause. The more contextual information troubleshooters receive from a problem report, the better able they are to discern potential causes of the problem and what steps may be required for diagnosis and resolution.

What contextual information does a troubleshooter require? In a perfect world, a problem report would answer the five questions of who, what, where, when, and how (Talbott and Zmau 2018):

> *Who reported the issue?* Is it an internal or external reporter? What is that person's affiliation and account status?
> *What is the issue?* Can the reporter describe what happened? Is it a patron-focused or technology-focused issue or both?
> *Where did the issue occur?* Where was the reporter located, both physically and electronically, when the issue occurred?
> *When did the issue occur?* What is the time frame for the issue? Did it happen multiple times over several days?
> *How was the issue encountered?* What steps did the reporter take before encountering the issue? What access tools were used? (65)

Challenges with Problem Reporting

Libraries face two big challenges when it comes to soliciting problem reports. The first concerns motivation. A troubleshooter would consider any break in access a problem that needs addressing, but this is not always true for potential reporters. External reporters are primarily concerned with filling their information needs, and access issues, while annoying, do not necessarily prevent them from doing so. For instance, a patron may encounter a broken link when trying to reach an article; however, the same article may be available from another platform, with its link located directly below the first on the same record. Having successfully accessed the article using the second link, the patron has achieved the goal and, as a result, will have less incentive to report the initial broken link. To increase the likelihood that a reporter will submit a problem report, libraries need to make reporting mechanisms as painless as possible, focusing on speed, convenience, and user-friendly interfaces.

The second challenge involves capturing enough information to accurately understand the problem. Problem reports seldom contain the answers to all five questions (who, what, where, when, and how) when they are first submitted. Reporters frequently do not know what contextual information is relevant to include or are unable to take the time to thoroughly document the issue. As a result, initial problem reports are often too vague to effectively troubleshoot. In his article on troubleshooting in a web-scale discovery environment, Todd Enoch (2018) highlights this exact challenge:

> [I]t was difficult for our users to consistently provide enough information. . . . Many librarians encountered problems in the midst of a reference interview or bibliographic instruction session and were unable to take the time necessary to capture all of the metadata concerning the problem link. By the time they were finished with their task, they typically found it difficult to recall or reproduce the exact problem well enough to report it. (2)

Libraries have attempted to mitigate this issue through both education and technology, working to train potential reporters on good reporting practices as well as expanding their problem report submission forms with more fields in order to capture the who, what, where, when, and how. However, it is important to remember that as the requirements for submission increase, it becomes more and more unlikely that reporters will be able or willing to meet them, resulting in fewer submissions. This is especially true for patrons and other external reporters, who may be intimidated by complex forms and mystifying library jargon. Instead, a balance needs to be struck between soliciting enough information to reach a resolution and not placing an undue burden on reporters.

One method of balancing these concerns is to create separate submission mechanisms for external and internal reporters. External reporters typically have only cursory knowledge of the library's technical systems; therefore, they are much more limited in how they understand and report access issues. The focus for these reporters should be on ease of submission, that is, reporting mechanisms that are readily available, easy to understand, and quick to complete. Beyond the standard communication methods of phone, e-mail, and chat, many libraries take advantage of opportunities to insert either contact information or "Report a problem" buttons throughout their access tools, including their discovery services, A–Z lists, and catalogs. If directing reporters to an online form, libraries have worked to simplify the required fields as much as possible, some even utilizing automated methods to collect the submitter's IP address, browser version, or resource citation information to increase convenience for the reporter while providing accurate information for the troubleshooter. Regardless of the submission method, the foremost goal is to open a dialogue with the reporters. Once the dialogue is established, more detailed information can be collected during the follow-up conversation.

By contrast, internal reporters are likely to be more familiar with the mechanisms that provide access than are libraries' patrons, and they generally have both the time and incentive to provide detailed reports about what went wrong. For these reporters, a stronger emphasis should be placed on receiving accurate and complete information upfront. Some libraries provide expanded reporting forms for their frontline staff to fill out as well as training on what information is relevant and why it needs to be collected. Training on problem report submission is especially important, as Katherine A. Hart and Tammy S. Sugarman (2016) explain: "[T]he authors realized the questions might be skipped if their significance was not understood. Drawing a connection between the questions and the interdependent e-resources systems would reinforce the importance of providing full answers to the questions" (30–31). See figures 3.1 and 3.2 for example problem report submission forms.

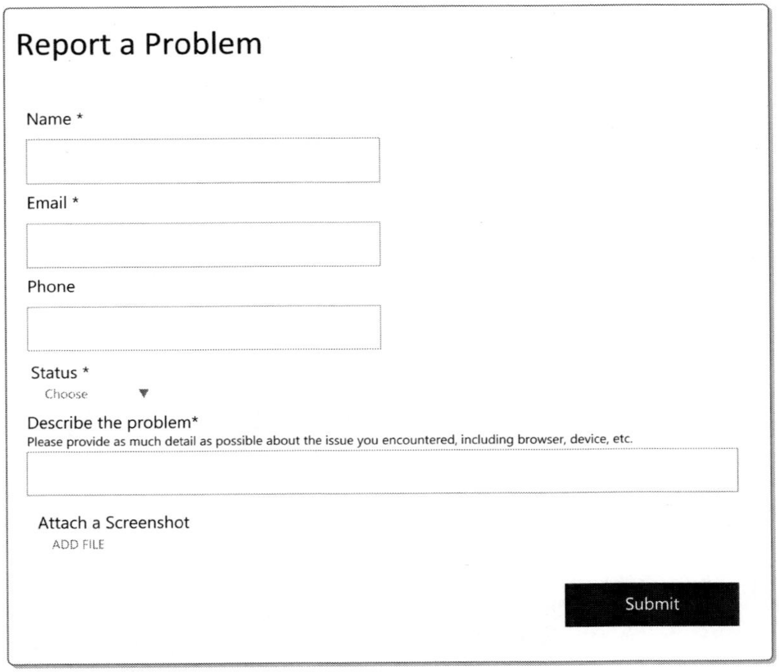

FIGURE 3.1
Simple problem report form

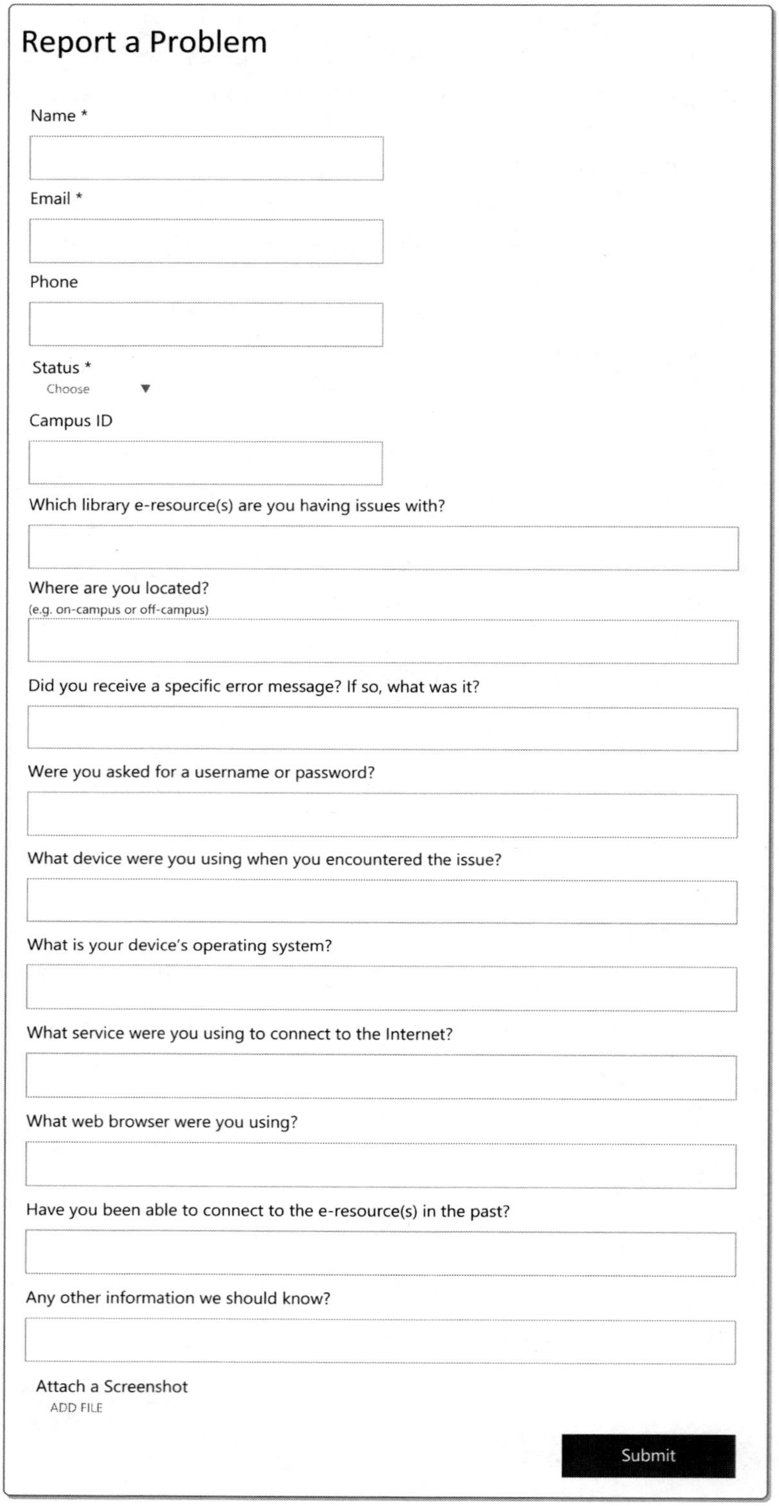

Report a Problem

Name *

Email *

Phone

Status *
Choose   ▼

Campus ID

Which library e-resource(s) are you having issues with?

Where are you located?
(e.g. on-campus or off-campus)

Did you receive a specific error message? If so, what was it?

Were you asked for a username or password?

What device were you using when you encountered the issue?

What is your device's operating system?

What service were you using to connect to the Internet?

What web browser were you using?

Have you been able to connect to the e-resource(s) in the past?

Any other information we should know?

Attach a Screenshot
ADD FILE

Submit

FIGURE 3.2
Expanded problem report form

Training is also important because many internal reporters submit tickets to troubleshooting staff on behalf of their patrons. Because successful ticket resolution is largely dependent on the amount and quality of the data provided to the troubleshooter, it is crucial that the internal reporters understand what to ask the patron and why in order to collect enough helpful information for the troubleshooter to resolve the issue. Otherwise, it can quickly become like a bad game of telephone, with the intermediary passing along a message that is incomprehensible to the listener on the other end. We discuss training for internal reporters further in chapter 7.

The Troubleshooting Interview

Expressing access issues in accurate, technical terms does not come naturally to patrons. Even with extensive experience, patrons will never obtain mastery over the plethora of e-resources or their access mechanisms. As a result, problem reports submitted by external reporters often do not contain enough information to diagnose and resolve access issues, requiring troubleshooters to open a dialogue with the reporters in order to obtain the missing information.

When engaging in this dialogue, we have found it helpful to approach it as one might a reference interview. A reference interview is simply a conversation between a patron with an information need and a librarian who seeks to both clarify and meet that need. At the start of a reference interview, the patron may state an information need in very broad terms, such as "I need articles about WWII." However, after a few open-ended questions about the context of the request (and what search strategies the patron has tried), the librarian may realize that the information need is actually this: "I need peer-reviewed articles on the effects of wartime propaganda on soldier enlistments in order to write a position paper for class."

Similarly, when reporting an access issue, a reporter may begin with a broad statement, such as "I can't access any library resources" or "Links to the *New England Journal of Medicine* are broken." It is then up to the troubleshooter to clarify the details of the issue by asking open-ended, contextual questions and discussing any resolution strategies the reporter has already tried. Through this process, the access issue may be narrowed to "The patron cannot access e-resources while using the VPN off campus" or "The link to the NEJM on the nursing research guide is broken." Because of the similarities to the reference interview, we have decided to call this conversation the troubleshooting interview.

The goal of the troubleshooting interview is to answer the five questions we discussed earlier—who, what, where, when, and how (henceforth abbreviated to 4W1H)—in as much depth as possible. What questions are asked and in what order will vary depending on the particular scenario. In the following list, we expound upon 4W1H and give some examples of open-ended questions to ask.

Who reported the issue? For external reporters, be sure to get the person's name, library status (current cardholder, visitor, graduate student, etc.), and contact information. Also, be sure to verify that the reporter has an active account with your institution. Not only do you need this information to respond with a solution or explanation, but it can also provide vital clues for troubleshooting. For internal reporters, you likely already have access to this information; however, you will need to discover if they are submitting the problem report on behalf of a patron. If they are, be sure to get that patron's name, library status, and contact information.

What is the issue? Get a detailed explanation of the problem. What e-resource(s) was the reporter trying to access? Try to get a citation or unique identifier. If the reporter encountered an error message, what did it say? Ask to see a screenshot. What is the context for accessing the e-resource? Is it for a class or project? Is the reporter able to access other library resources? You will want to verify any broad statements. The aim here is to delineate the scope of the problem as much as possible, with a focus on identifying whether it is a patron-focused problem, a technology-focused problem, or both.

Where did the issue occur? Find out where the reporter was located, both physically and electronically, when the issue occurred. Was the reporter at home? On a library computer? On a cell phone at the airport? Pay particular attention to what kinds of device, browser, and internet connection the reporter was using, as these can all affect access.

When did the issue occur? Find out the time frame for the issue. When did it occur? Is this the first incident or a recurring problem? Timing of the issue can sometimes offer an explanation (e.g., it occurred during scheduled server downtime) or give you a handle on how persistent the issue is.

How was the issue encountered? Ask reporters to retrace their steps. Troubleshooters should attempt to retrace the steps alongside the reporters. How did they get to the access issue? Where did they start from? What access tool were they using? What links did they click on? What prompts did they encounter? The more you can visualize a reporter's journey, the easier it is to re-create the problem.

Like the reference interview, a troubleshooting interview is more of an art than a science. While detailed information about access issues helps to illuminate possible resolutions, peppering reporters with questions or replying to problem reports with ever-expanding requests for details can be off-putting and may cause reporters to disengage. With time and experience, troubleshooters will get better at identifying what questions to ask and when as well as recognizing what answers from reporters require a deeper line of inquiry. However, bearing in mind some basic customer service etiquette can help ease the way, keeping a reporter invested while the troubleshooter works through the issue.

Etiquette is important when interacting with both internal and external reporters. When applied well, etiquette can establish a positive and productive conversation, helping to manage expectations, diffuse frustration, and increase the likelihood that a reporter will submit problem reports in the future. Always keep in mind the basics: be polite, be empathetic, be responsive, and always think before you speak or type. Remember that written words do not have the benefit of voice tone or body language, and so they can be easily misunderstood or mis-interpreted by the recipient. Therefore, it is always better to err on the side of politeness.

When working with external reporters, it is important to focus first on iden-tifying and filling their immediate information needs (i.e., solving the patron-focused problem). In terms of 4W1H, this means primarily focusing on the who (are they authorized users?), the what (which resource are they after and why?), and the how (how were they trying to access the resource?). Once the resource has been pinpointed and the reporter verified as an authorized user, a troubleshooter should endeavor to send the desired resource to the reporter or provide the reporter with an alternative means of accessing the content. Mak-ing a reporter wait to receive the content while the troubleshooter works on resolving the technology-focused problem is poor customer service. The sooner the troubleshooter can resolve the patron-focused problem, the better. However, we want to emphasize that a troubleshooter should not send materials directly to a reporter unless that person is an affiliated user and active account holder. We recommend troubleshooters send library materials only to the e-mail address associated with the reporter's active account.

Even if access to the resource cannot be provided immediately, a trouble-shooter should not leave the reporter at a dead end. For example, if a problem report's resolution depends on fixing a back-end technology issue, the trouble-shooter should determine if the patron's information need can be met only by the original, desired resource or if it could be met by a different, comparable resource. In practical terms, the patron may simply need to be directed to interlibrary loan to request the original resource or referred to a subject specialist who can aid the patron in discovering alternative resources.

Here are a few other points of etiquette to keep in mind when corresponding with external reporters:

- In the initial contact with external reporters, reassure them that their problem report has been received and will be addressed. Many institutions make it a point of replying to a problem report within twenty-four hours to assure the reporter that the issue is being worked on.
- Avoid using too much library jargon when discussing issues with external reporters. Although a reporter may appreciate an explanation about what went wrong, using too many unfamiliar terms will result in confusion rather than clarity. If library jargon is unavoidable, provide explanations for terms the reporter may not know.
- Manage expectations when informing a patron of a potential timeline for resolution of the problem report. Trust your instincts and explain up front that the patron may need to use interlibrary loan or seek out alternative resources.
- When directing patrons to the reference or interlibrary loan department, provide them with the necessary information to contact these staff and be prepared to answer any questions they may have about how a reference interview or an interlibrary loan request works. We discuss problem report follow-up in detail in chapter 5.

Internal reporters differ from external reporters in that they are less likely to have an immediate information access need. Internal reporters may come across access issues in the course of their daily work, but unless they are submitting the problem report on behalf of a patron or are engaged in an activity that requires a specific resource (e.g., a class or one-on-one reference session), they do not necessarily need to gain access to the resource itself. The act of submitting the problem report is mostly to ensure that future users are not denied access, rather than coming from a desire to use the resource themselves. As a result, internal reporters may be less invested in receiving a resolution. This, of course, will vary depending on the reporter and the issue at hand, but in many instances internal reporters consider their job done once the problem report has been submitted. For these reasons, we recommend focusing on thoroughly defining the technology-focused problem during the troubleshooting interview.

Example Scenarios

Let's look at some examples of answering the 4W1H questions during a troubleshooting interview. We will return to the scenarios in this section in chapters 4 and 5 when we discuss diagnosing and resolving access issues; therefore, in this chapter, we cover only identifying the problem and examining the situation for each of the following three scenarios.

SCENARIO 1

A troubleshooter receives the following ticket within the library's help ticket system:

> July 24, 2019, 08:38 a.m. via Online Form Submission
> Name: Janet Roe
> E-mail: jroe@email.university.edu
> Status: Graduate student
> Message: I can't get to the article "Platyhelminth models for stem-cell research" by Hepzibah Smith. The links in the library search are all broken: https://university-search.hosted.discoveryvendor.com/permalink/f/1h1j3k/TN_JournalofBiology/doi0220111

From the problem report, the troubleshooter knows the following things:

Who: The reporter is a graduate student; by looking up the student's account information using the provided e-mail, the troubleshooter can learn the student's account status; in this case, the student's account is active and in good standing.

What: The student was trying to access an article titled "Platyhelminth Models for Stem-Cell Research" by Hepzibah Smith; by looking at the URL the student provided, the troubleshooter knows it is an article in the *Journal of Biology*; more complete citation information may be gathered by visiting the URL, which is a permalink to a discovery record.

Where: The problem report does not specify if the student was on or off campus when trying to access the article; more follow-up may be required.

When: The problem report specifies only when the report was submitted, in this case 8:38 a.m.; however, it is likely that the student reported the access issue shortly after encountering it.

How: The student states that the issue was encountered in the "library search"; paired with the URL the student provided, the troubleshooter knows that the student encountered the issue within the library's discovery service.

Based on this information, the troubleshooter is able to identify both the patron-focused and the technology-focused problem. The patron-focused problem is that the student could not access the specified article. The easiest way to solve this problem would be to offer access to the article either by providing an alternative route to the article or by sending the article to the student's institutional e-mail address. If access cannot be provided immediately, the troubleshooter may want to further clarify the information need and then refer the student either to interlibrary loan or to a subject liaison to find other resources that could fill the need. In this case, the troubleshooter was able to access the article by navigating to the *Journal of Biology* through the library's e-journal A–Z list and then searching for the correct article.

The technology-focused problem is that the article links on the record are "broken." The troubleshooter is very fortunate that the reporter provided the permalink to the discovery record. Using the permalink, the troubleshooter is able to go to the exact record the patron encountered and try the links firsthand. It turns out that two links are displayed on the record—one for a backfile journal package and one for a science journal package from the same vendor—both of which result in the message "No results found" when clicked. To fix this problem, the troubleshooter would need to discover why these links are broken. We cover diagnosing and resolving tickets in the next two chapters.

To: <jroe@email.university.edu>
From: <troubleshooting@email.university.edu>
July 24, 2019, 09:02 a.m.

Hello Janet,
I'm sorry you are having difficulty accessing this article. I also tested the links and they are not working for me as well. While we work on getting them fixed, I have included instructions on how you can navigate to the article without using the links. Please see the instructions below.

SCENARIO 2

A library staff member engages in the following chat:

8.30.2019 | 3:04 p.m.
   Apatel3: Hi, I'm trying to read an article online but it says I have to pay to view it.

Once again, the initial message does not contain much information to answer the 4W1H questions. The troubleshooter will want to focus first on discovering *what* article the reporter is after in order to begin solving the patron-focused problem. The reporter will also want to gather some more contextual information about *how* the article was accessed and *where* the reporter was located to determine if a technology issue exists. In this instance, the troubleshooter chooses to focus on defining where the reporter is located.

> Librarian: Hello. I'm sorry you are having difficulties accessing the article. Could you tell me what one you are after? Are you on campus?
>
> Apatel3: Use of flipped classrooms in higher education by O'Flaherty.
>
> Apatel3: I'm at home.
>
> Librarian: Is it this one in the *Journal of Education*? https://university -search.hosted.discoveryvendor.com/permalink/z/7p14s67/TN_ JournalofEducation/doi1148972
>
> Apatel3: Yeah that's it.
>
> Apatel3: I tried all the links but they say I have to pay.
>
> Librarian: Okay, one moment please.

The reporter provides enough citation information for the article that the troubleshooter is able to search and find it within the library's discovery service. When presented with a link to the record in the discovery service, the reporter verifies that it is not only the correct article but also the same record that she used to attempt to access it. This answers both *what* and part of *how*. Next, the troubleshooter attempts to access the article before deciding how best to address the patron's immediate need. In this case, the troubleshooter is also denied access to the article at the vendor's platform after trying the links on the record and by navigating to the article via the library's e-journal A–Z list.

> Librarian: I'm receiving the same message. I will need to look into this further, but it might take a little while to track down the problem. Could I have your name and university e-mail so I can let you know when it's fixed?
>
> Apatel3: Anaya Patel, apatel3@email.university.edu
>
> Apatel3: Do you know how long it'll take? I need it ASAP.
>
> Librarian: I'm not sure how long it will take to fix it. It will depend on what's wrong. Since you need the article ASAP, let's have you request it through interlibrary loan. This way you can get a copy while we work on restoring access. Most requests are filled within twenty-four hours.
>
> Librarian: Here's the form—https://library.university.edu/ILLrequestform
>
> Librarian: Let me know if you need help filling it out.
>
> Apatel3: Okay, thanks.

At this point, the troubleshooter has resolved the patron-focused problem and has enough answers to the 4W1H questions to begin diagnosing the technology-focused problem.

From the chat, the troubleshooter has defined 4W1H as follows:

Who: The reporter is an undergraduate student with an account in good standing.

What: The reporter cannot access the article "The Use of Flipped Classrooms in Higher Education" by O'Flaherty in the *Journal of Education*.

Where: The reporter is located off campus; the troubleshooter is located on campus.

When: Because this is a chat, the troubleshooter can presume the issue is happening right now.

How: The troubleshooter did not ask the reporter to retrace her steps; however, the troubleshooter discovered that navigating to the article through the links in the discovery service and by going to the journal through the library's e-journal A–Z list resulted in a paywall message.

In this scenario, the patron-focused problem is that the reporter cannot access a desired article in the *Journal of Education*. Although why the article is needed is not specified, the reporter does need it as soon as possible. The technology-focused problem is that the article is inaccessible because of a paywall on the vendor's platform.

SCENARIO 3

A troubleshooter receives the following e-mail:

> To: <troubleshooting@email.university.edu>
> From: <lehane@email.university.edu>
> Subject: Unable to View the Film Rashomon
>
> Hello,
> I was planning on showing the film *Rashomon* in my Cinema 107 class this semester, but when I went to view the video this weekend, I got a message saying the library doesn't subscribe to it anymore. I was able to show it last year. Did something change? I can't believe the library would cancel its subscription to such a seminal film!
>
> Kelsey LeHane, PhD
> Associate Professor
> School of Film, Theatre, and Television

From the initial problem report, the troubleshooter knows the following:

Who: The reporter is a faculty professor teaching a Cinema 107 class.
What: The reporter was attempting to access the film *Rashomon*.
When: The reporter was attempting to view the film the previous weekend.

The problem report does not mention *how* the reporter was attempting to access the video nor *where* the reporter was located.

Based on this information, the troubleshooter is able to identify the patron-focused problem: the reporter wants to show the 1950 Kurosawa film *Rashomon* in an upcoming Cinema 107 class but will be unable to do so because the reporter cannot access the film. However, there is not enough information for the troubleshooter to identify the technology-focused problem or even confirm whether one exists. As a next step, the troubleshooter will want to provide access to the film, if possible. The troubleshooter searches for the film in the library's discovery service and finds a record with a link to a popular film platform. Unfortunately, the troubleshooter is unable to view the film—it is as if the library's access has been cut, or perhaps the library does not truly have access to the video. After checking a few more video platforms to confirm the film is not available through another vendor, the troubleshooter concludes that the film is not available for immediate access.

To: <lehane@email.university.edu>
From: <troubleshooting@email.university.edu>
Subject: Re: Unable to View the Film Rashomon

Dear Dr. LeHane,
Thank you for reaching out about this issue. I want to confirm that this is the film you were attempting to view: https://proxy.yourlibrary.org/login?url=https://www.videoplatform.com/195002030

I am receiving the same subscription message when I try to watch the video. I will need to investigate to see why the message is appearing. I will e-mail you as soon as I have an update.

Kind regards,
Troubleshooter

To: <troubleshooting@email.university.edu>
From: <lehane@email.university.edu>
Subject: Re: Unable to View the Film Rashomon

Yes, that's the one. I need to know as soon as possible if I'll be able to show it in class. Otherwise I'll need to find another film!

Kelsey LeHane, PhD
Associate Professor
School of Film, Theatre, and Television

User Error

During the course of a troubleshooting interview, the troubleshooter may discover that there is no technology-focused problem to resolve. These instances are usually the result of user error, that is, the reporter incorrectly interpreting or utilizing the technologies that provide access. For example, a novice library user may not understand the various types of records available within a discovery service and report the full text of a book as missing when the record is for a book review instead. Similarly, a patron may report being denied access after navigating to an e-resource via an internet search engine instead of a library access tool.

Let's look at a couple scenarios and their resolutions.

SCENARIO 4

A troubleshooter receives the following e-mail:

To: <troubleshooting@email.university.edu>
From: <george@email.com>
Subject: Genealogy Database

Hi, I can't use the library's genealogy database. I could use it okay last weekend, but when I try logging in to it now, the website says I don't have an account. Can you help?

Thanks,
George Williamson

To: <george@email.com>
From: <troubleshooting@email.university.edu>
Subject: Re: Genealogy Database

Hi George,
Thank you for reaching out to us. You were trying to access this genealogy database, correct? https://proxy.yourlibrary.org/login?url=https://www .geneaologydatabase.com

I tested access and was able to get in and view the contents. Can you walk me through step-by-step how you were trying to access it? Does the link above work for you?

To: <troubleshooting@email.university.edu>
From: <george@email.com>
Subject: Re: Genealogy Database

Hi,
Yes, that link worked! Thank you! I got to the database by typing the name into Google. I clicked the website link and then clicked the log-in button at the top. I tried entering my library username and password, but it said it didn't recognize it. I used this database at the library last weekend and it didn't ask me for a password. Why doesn't my library one work?

To: <george@email.com>
From: <troubleshooting@email.university.edu>
Subject: Re: Genealogy Database

Hi George,
I'm glad to hear that the link I sent you worked. For most of our library resources, you do not have to log in to them if you are accessing them at the library. However, if you are not at the library, you will need to access them through the library website or through a specially formatted link, like the one I sent you. The database website will not recognize your log-in if you go directly there instead.

SCENARIO 5

A library staff member engages in the following chat:

11.21.2019 | 10:43 p.m.

Guest: Hi.

Librarian: Hello, how can I assist you today?

Guest: I'm trying to get an article but the link is broken.

Librarian: Let's see if I can help. What article are you trying to view?

Guest: Colonialism and the Figurative Strategy of Jane Eyre

Librarian: Okay, and where did you find the link? Can you describe what happens when you click it? Do you get an error message?

Guest: I found it in the library search. I can see the title and everything, but when I click it, it just expands the information. It doesn't go to the PDF.

Guest: And there's no other links to click.

Librarian: One moment please.

Librarian: I do see a record for this article in the library search. Is this the right one? https://university-search.hosted.discoveryvendor.com/permalink/z/9zp24/a559

Guest: Yes, that's it.

Librarian: I do see what you mean about there not being any PDF links on the record.

Librarian: This is a citation-only record, which means there is no full text attached to it. The library includes records like these for items we don't own or subscribe to, but that people may want to search for. You can tell citation-only records because of the label at the top that says "Journal Article: Citation Online."

Guest: Okay, so I can't get the article?

Librarian: You will need to put in a request for it through interlibrary loan. They are usually pretty fast about getting the articles to you.

Librarian: Here is the form—https://library.university.edu/ILLrequestform

Guest: Okay, thanks.

Librarian: Is there anything else I can help you with today?

Guest: No, that's it.

In each of these cases, no corrections to the library system are necessary. The problem is resolved once the reporters have been educated about the misunderstandings and assisted in filling their information needs.

Conclusion

No matter the submission method, the more contextual information troubleshooters receive from a problem report, the better able they are to discern potential causes of the problem and what steps may be required for diagnosis and resolution. Soliciting contextual information from patrons is a careful balance of variables, including reviewing information in the required fields of an online problem report form, asking just enough questions during a troubleshooting interview, and employing professional etiquette when communicating with patrons who may be frustrated by their access issues. Education on reporting for both internal and external reporters is also necessary to successfully solicit enough information for a troubleshooter to accurately define a problem and examine the situation. Without a technology-focused problem to define, problem reports that result from user error simply require patrons to be educated about their misunderstandings to be resolved. Once 4W1H, the patron-focused problem, and the technology-focused problem of a given problem report are defined, a troubleshooter can then proceed to consider the possible causes and solutions of a given problem report, which we discuss in chapter 4.

ADDITIONAL READINGS AND RESOURCES

Brûlé, Anne. 2009. "Troubleshooting Access to Electronic Resources." *Access* 15 (4): 12–13.

Donlan, Rebecca. 2007. "Boulevard of Broken Links: Keeping Users Connected to E-journal Content." *Reference Librarian* 48 (1): 99–104.

Graham, Tess, and Nate Hosburgh. 2014. "A User-Centered Approach to Addressing Issues of Discoverability and Access." *Serials Librarian* 67 (1): 48–51.

Perkins, Jeffrey. 2008. "Solving Electronic Journal Problems Effectively: A Short Guide." *Journal of Electronic Resources in Medical Libraries* 5 (3): 267–73. doi:10.1080/15424060802222471.

Ross, Sheri V. T., and Sarah W. Sutton. 2016. "Providing Access to Electronic Resources." In *Guide to Electronic Resource Management*, 69–92. Santa Barbara, CA: Libraries Unlimited.

REFERENCES

Enoch, Todd. 2018. "Tracking Down the Problem: The Development of a Web-Scale Discovery Troubleshooting Workflow." *Serials Librarian* 74 (1–4): 234–39. doi:10.1080/0361526X.2018.1427984.

Hart, Katherine A., and Tammy S. Sugarman. 2016. "Developing an Interdepartmental Training Program for E-resources Troubleshooting." *Serials Librarian* 71 (1): 25–38. doi:10.1080/0361526X.2016.1169569.

Smith, Mike U. 1991. *Toward a Unified Theory of Problem Solving: Views from the Content Domains*. Hillsdale, NJ: Lawrence Erlbaum.

Talbott, Holly, and Ashley Zmau. 2018. "The Help Desk." In *Electronic Resources Librarianship: A Practical Guide for Librarians*, 63–80. Lanham, MD: Rowman & Littlefield.

4

Diagnosing Access Issues

Once a troubleshooter has received a report of an access issue and per-formed an initial examination of the situation, it is time to commence the next step in the troubleshooting process: identifying the possible causes of the access issue by examining the symptoms being displayed. Unlike the previous steps in the troubleshooting process, which focus equally on the patron-focused problem and technology-focused problem, diagnosing is chiefly concentrated on a library's access technology and how it is or is not functioning rather than on fulfilling a patron's information need. The purpose is to determine why the access issue occurred based on the evidence presented and to begin formulating possible solutions.

Before we dive into the various causes and symptoms of access issues, we want to remind you that diagnosing, like troubleshooting itself, is not a linear path. As library technology becomes more complex and interdependent, uncovering the cause of any access issue becomes more difficult. Many times, distinct causes will express themselves in similar ways, such as broken links, 404 error messages, or paywalls, making them challenging to pinpoint. Other times, the issue experienced by a patron is not the result of a single root cause but of the commingling of several malfunctions along the access chain. As a result, diagnosing can be a recursive process, with troubleshooters returning to gather additional information or context, if their first diagnosis proves to be inaccurate.

In this chapter, we revisit the concept of the access chain and delve deeper into its various components to discuss how and why access interruptions happen and how a troubleshooter can work to identify the cause (or causes) of the disruptions based on the symptoms presented. Along the way, we talk about some strategies that troubleshooters can use to further refine their diagnoses and tips and tricks to try if they get stuck.

Reproducible versus Unreproducible Problems

You will recall from chapter 2 the concept of a library access chain, or the chain of interconnected technologies a patron moves through in order to access a library resource. A library may have several access chains through which a patron can obtain electronic resources, and which, when combined, form a comprehensive overview of the library's access system. Many of these access chains are composed of similar components, such as a link resolver, proxy server, and vendor platform, and can be powered by several sources of metadata, including catalogs, knowledge bases, and central indexes. We have mapped out several access chains in figure 4.1 that we will refer to throughout this chapter.

The basic components that comprise an access chain also fall into one of four spheres of control: patron controlled, library controlled, vendor controlled, or blended control. This means, depending on whose sphere of control the component falls under, a troubleshooter will have a greater or lesser ability to test hypotheses, effect change, and enact solutions. Although this knowledge is especially necessary during the next phase of troubleshooting—considering the possible solutions and implementing a solution—understanding the different spheres of control can also assist with diagnosis because it affects how and where particular symptoms will be displayed within the chain.

For instance, whether the source of an access issue is within a patron-controlled component or within a library- or vendor-controlled component will affect whether the troubleshooter is able to reproduce the issue. The very first troubleshooting strategy we recommend all troubleshooters try when diagnosing an access issue is re-creation, or reproducing the symptoms/failure based on a set procedure or sequence of steps. Usually, this means re-creating the steps the reporter took before encountering the access issue in order to see whether the troubleshooter experiences the same symptoms.

As a general rule of thumb, reproducible problems indicate the cause of the breakdown is within the library-controlled or vendor-controlled part of the access chain. This makes sense, of course. If an issue is presenting itself to multiple users (in this case, the reporter and the troubleshooter) who are employing different devices, browsers, and network settings, the issue is likely unrelated to these patron-specific components. There are exceptions to this rule, of course, mostly in regard to browsers and browser settings, which can be reproduced if the troubleshooter is given enough information.

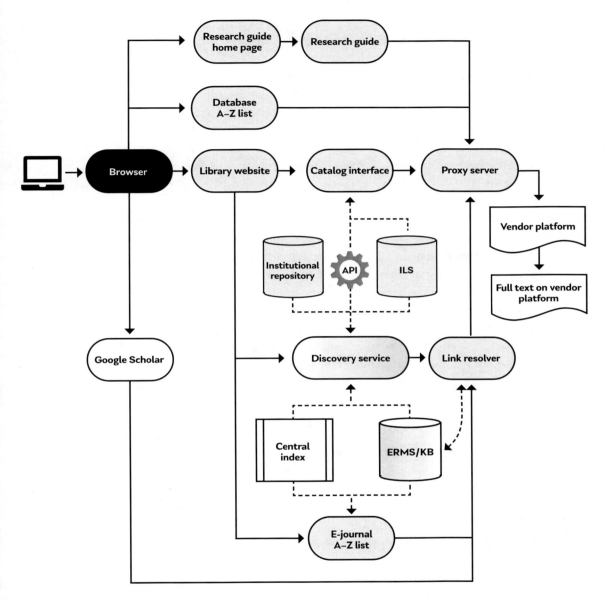

FIGURE 4.1
Comprehensive access chain

Unreproducible problems, on the other hand, typically indicate an issue with the patron-controlled part of the access chain. However, this statement comes with a huge caveat: the reporter must have provided the troubleshooter with enough information to accurately replicate the access chain that the reporter followed. If a troubleshooter is forced to guess or make assumptions about the components based on incomplete information, then the fact that the troubleshooter was unable to re-create the issue may simply mean that the troubleshooter guessed incorrectly.

The wildcard here is authentication. When problems arise during the authentication process, the symptoms sometimes can and sometimes cannot be reproduced. As we discussed in chapter 2, authentication can happen at various points along the access chain and through various methods. While these points and methods may be decided upon and managed by the library and the vendor (i.e., if authentication is able to happen via username/password, IP address, proxy server, VPN, or single sign-on), the specifics of authentication, including when, where, and how it occurs, are primarily dependent on the patrons, their actions, and their physical locations.

For example, let's imagine two patrons navigating to the same database from off campus. Both choose to access the database through the same route: going to the library's website, selecting the database A–Z list, and clicking the proxied link under the appropriate entry. The first patron, whose IP address is identified by the proxy as being off campus, is presented with the institution's sign-in screen after clicking the database link and must enter credentials before being redirected to the database platform. The second patron, by contrast, is a faculty member in the habit of using the institution's VPN whenever performing research while off campus and so has already launched the VPN application before navigating to the library website. Because the VPN's IP address is identified by the proxy as being on campus, the patron is not presented with a sign-in screen before being directed to the database platform.

Now, let's imagine these patrons encounter a paywall once they reach the database platform and reach out to the library for help. The troubleshooter would dutifully attempt to re-create the route taken by the patrons by going to the library website, selecting the database A–Z list, and clicking on the proxied link; however, because the troubleshooter is located within the library, the IP address is identified by the proxy as being on campus and the troubleshooter is not presented with the institution's sign-in screen. Instead, the troubleshooter is immediately directed to the database platform. While all three navigated to the database through the same route and were authenticated through methods created and controlled by the library and vendor, the individual actions and physical locations of each person made a significant difference in how each one was authenticated. As a result of this blended control, a troubleshooter's ability to accurately replicate a patron's experience—and thus access issues related to authentication—will vary widely.

To limit this variability, many troubleshooters employ tools to help mimic a patron's particular actions or circumstances. For example, some libraries create guest or dummy accounts for troubleshooters with the settings and restrictions of specific patron types, such as undergraduate or graduate students, faculty members, or walk-in patrons. Troubleshooters may also use VPNs, proxy websites, or browser extensions meant for anonymizing web traffic to hide their on-campus IP addresses and thus receive the same authentication prompts as remote patrons. Of course, these tools are not foolproof, and the absence of described symptoms while using these tools does not necessarily rule out authentication as the origin of the issue. However, the closer troubleshooters can get to replicating a reporter's actions and circumstances, the better able they are to test their hypotheses.

Patron-Controlled Components: Common Issues and Their Symptoms

An access chain always begins with patron-controlled components, namely, the patron's device, internet or network connection, and browser and browser settings. Access issues originating within these components can present symptoms anywhere throughout the access chain, but they are most typically felt at either the beginning of the chain or toward the end. Also, the symptoms frequently cannot be reproduced by the troubleshooter, which can make diagnosing the issue quite difficult. The following list presents some common causes and symptoms originating from each component:

> *Device:* The patron's device is running an old or unsupported operating system; the patron's device does not have the appropriate software for viewing or interacting with the library resource (e.g., does not have a PDF viewer or reader with DRM [digital rights management] software, such as Adobe Digital Editions, installed). Symptoms include slow upload and download times and the inability to open or view downloaded file types.
>
> *Network and internet connectivity:* The patron's network connection is slow, is spotty, or experiences high latency (delays in transmitting and processing network data; this is common with satellite internet); the patron's satellite internet service provider's proxy or VPN (used to mitigate latency issues) interacts negatively with the library's authentication system (e.g., EZproxy). Symptoms include timeout errors, lag, slow upload and download times, and dropped proxy or authentication.

Browser and browser settings: The patron is using an older browser or a browser unsupported by the vendor platform; the data stored in the browser's cache or cookies is interacting negatively with the vendor platform or library resource; the browser's pop-up blocker is preventing content from loading; or the browser's security settings are blocking safe sites from being accessed. Symptoms include slow loading times, content or web pages not loading on the vendor platform, and error messages or security warnings.

Because access issues originating from patron-controlled components are particular to the patron's device setup and require action by the patron to be resolved, it is best to test for them early in the troubleshooting process. The simplest way is to have the patron remove or replace each of these components from the access chain—a technique called *elimination*—thus excluding them as possible causes. This could mean asking patrons to use a different device or browser, to clear their browser's cache and cookies, to disable any advertising or pop-up blockers, or to modify their security settings. This also means being aware of any compatibility issues or software requirements for specific vendor platforms. If a vendor platform is not compatible with mobile devices or can be accessed using only certain browser versions or DRM software, the troubleshooter should first check that the patron is meeting these requirements before diving into additional problem solving.

Given that many of these issues can be resolved through simple, quick changes, many libraries choose to run through these basic checks—like changing browsers and clearing caches and cookies—during every troubleshooting interview, regardless of whether the symptoms indicate a need. By doing so, either the access issue will be resolved quickly or the troubleshooter will know to eliminate those components as possible causes. In addition, some libraries provide self-help guides for patrons and frontline staff to test for and resolve these technology issues themselves. These guides include such helpful information as how to clear caches and cookies, edit browser security settings, reset passwords, or successfully use a finicky platform. Libraries also try to proactively assist patrons by utilizing the note and display features available through some access tools to indicate software or browser requirements.

Troubleshooting Tip: Incognito Mode

Did you know you can use incognito mode to test whether a browser's cache, cookies, or browsing history is interfering with access? This feature is referred to as Incognito Mode in Chrome, Private Browsing in Firefox, InPrivate Browsing in Internet Explorer and Microsoft Edge, and Private Window in Safari. Incognito mode works by creating a separate, "clean" session within a browser, free from any previously stored web data. This allows troubleshooters to effectively clear their caches and cookies without actually losing any of the information.

Sources and Types of Metadata

A significant portion of e-resource troubleshooting is derived from incorrect metadata. As we discussed in chapter 2, bibliographic, holdings, and location information form the backbone of all library access and linking tools. This means any missing, erroneous, or out-of-date metadata will adversely affect the discoverability of an e-resource and potentially lead to breakdowns in access. However, metadata can originate from a number of sources, including internally within the library or externally with a publisher, content provider, or discovery vendor. It is also often blended together within individual access tools, making it difficult to pinpoint where the metadata came from, what portion is causing the issue, and which party is responsible for correcting it. Understanding the flow of metadata from its various origination points is therefore essential. Within this environment of shared data, successful troubleshooting always asks early on, "Where is this metadata coming from?"

In table 4.1, we have summarized the sources and types of metadata that feed into each component in the access chain. We have also included a rough guide to whose sphere of control each falls under: library, vendor, or a blend of the two. This table is solely focused on e-resource metadata and therefore does not account for other sources of print, digital, or institutional repository metadata. Also, please note that the table is not exhaustive and represents only metadata that we have found to be the most commonly used for troubleshooting e-resources. Depending on your particular access tools, the sources, types, and spheres of control may be different.

TABLE 4.1 Sources and types of metadata

Component	Sources of Metadata	Types of Metadata	Sphere of Control
Online catalog/ILS	• Original MARC record cataloging • Individual MARC record loads • Bulk MARC record loads	• Bibliographic metadata • Database/collection citation metadata • Book citation metadata • Journal citation metadata • Video citation metadata • URLs	Library
Discovery interface	• Online catalog/ILS • APIs	• Bibliographic metadata • Database/collection citation metadata • Book citation metadata • Journal citation metadata • Video citation metadata • URLs	Blended
Central index	• Data supplied by publishers, vendors, and content providers	• Bibliographic metadata • Video citation metadata • Article citation metadata • Abstracts • Full text • Direct links • DOIs (digital object identifiers) • Tables of contents	Vendor
Knowledge base	• Data supplied by publishers, vendors, and content providers	• Bibliographic metadata • Database/collection citation metadata • Book citation metadata • Journal citation metadata • Video citation metadata • Parser and parser parameters • Link resolver information	Vendor
Web-scale discovery service	• Online catalog/ILS • Central index • Knowledge base • APIs	• Bibliographic metadata • Database/collection citation metadata • Book citation metadata • Journal citation metadata • Video citation metadata • Article citation metadata • Abstracts • Full text • Direct links • DOIs	Blended

Component	Sources of Metadata	Types of Metadata	Sphere of Control
Library services platform	• Original MARC record cataloging • Individual MARC record loads • Bulk MARC record loads • Knowledge base	• Bibliographic metadata • Database/collection citation metadata • Book citation metadata • Journal citation metadata • Video citation metadata • Parser and parser parameters • Link resolver information • Site IDs	Blended
Link resolver	• Knowledge base	• Citation information • Parser and parser parameters • Link resolver information	Vendor
ERMS	• Selection of holdings from a knowledge base	• Bibliographic metadata • Database/collection citation metadata • Book citation metadata • Journal citation metadata • Video citation metadata • Site IDs	Blended
Database A–Z list	• Manual record creation	• Database/collection title • URLs	Library
E-journal A–Z list	• Autopopulated from holdings selected from a knowledge base	• Journal citation metadata • Holdings/coverage dates • URLs	Blended
Research guide	• Manual entry • Asset management tool	• Database/collection title • Book title • Journal title • Video title • URLs	Library

The three main reservoirs of metadata that power library access tools are catalogs, knowledge bases, and central indexes. Access disruptions originating from a library's catalog or ILS generally concern locally controlled MARC records that contain incorrect or incomplete bibliographic information, coverage dates, or URLs. MARC records may have also been unwittingly loaded or unsuppressed for content the library does not currently own or subscribe to. When patrons encounter metadata from these faulty MARC records within an access tool (e.g., a discovery interface or discovery service), they may experience broken links, proxy error messages, missing or unnecessary prompts for authentication, or paywalls on the vendor platform. Fortunately, once the problem is isolated to the appropriate MARC record, a troubleshooter is able to take swift action to resolve the issue because these records are typically managed by the library itself. This is often not true when it comes to knowledge bases and central indexes.

Unlike a catalog, a knowledge base contains more than just bibliographic metadata; it also contains data that describes specific instances of e-resources, including the resource's platform, vendor, coverage dates, and access model, such as which packages or collections it appears in. Because the knowledge base receives this data directly from publishers or content providers, each of whom has its own internal standards for representing e-resource information, the quality of the metadata can vary from provider to provider. Some knowledge base vendors attempt to augment or normalize this data in order to keep it consistent across providers, but this process can also introduce additional errors. Furthermore, providers frequently make changes to their platforms, the content of those platforms, and the way that content is packaged and sold to libraries, making it difficult for knowledge base vendors to keep up with the changes. As a result, there is often a lag time between when a collection or resource is modified on the provider's platform and when its metadata is modified within the knowledge base. This can result in scenarios such as the following:

- broken links caused by outdated URLs or incorrect linking information
- broken links caused by incorrect bibliographic/citation information (e.g., wrong ISSN/ISBN)
- links defaulting to a provider's homepage instead of the individual article/title
- packages missing titles that have been added
- packages including inaccessible titles or titles that have been removed

Because a knowledge base is often utilized in a number of access chain components, including ERMSs, discovery services, link resolvers, and e-journal A–Z lists, these symptoms can display in several places. This means testing access via different access tools may result in the same error message or broken link. Not only does this limit the alternative routes troubleshooters can provide to problem reporters for accessing their desired content, but it also prevents troubleshooters from cross-checking the metadata within the library's access infrastructure. Instead, troubleshooters will need to do that through an outside source, such as OCLC or Ulrich's Periodicals Directory, or by going directly to the vendor or resource itself.

Missing, erroneous, and outdated metadata is also the primary cause of access issues originating from a central index. Like a knowledge base, a central index ingests metadata from hundreds of publishers and content providers, each of which has its own standards for representing e-resource metadata. This means the metadata quality often varies according to who is providing it and suffers from issues similar to those of a knowledge base regarding normalization, missing content, and lag time between when a resource is modified on a platform and when it is updated within the index. However, unlike a knowledge base, a central index is primarily used to provide discoverability for the smaller, individual pieces comprising a larger work, such as articles, abstracts, book chapters, images, video segments, and so on. This distinction is important to remember because a knowledge base and a central index express similar symptoms—most typically, broken or misdirecting links—when their metadata is faulty, but the issue may need to be reported to a different vendor or support portal, depending on which company the library has contracted with for each. It is often easiest to identify whom to contact based on what type of discovery record is experiencing the problem.

Troubleshooting Tip: Origin of Source Record

Did you know that discovery services often display the origin of their source records within the search interface? In Primo, for instance, the source (e.g., local MARC record, knowledge base collection, or central index collection) is often listed under the Details section of the discovery record. Similarly, in EBSCO Discovery Service (EDS), the source is usually listed under Database on the details page. EDS also provides the ability to enable a link to the MARC record. These features vary by discovery service and may need to be enabled on the backend, so if you do not see this option, talk with your discovery service administrator.

Troubleshooting Tip: MARC Record Source

Did you know that the source of a MARC record is often indicated within the record itself? When evaluating a MARC record to determine if its origins are local or from your knowledge base, look for an additional unique identifier in the 0XX fields (e.g., 020, 022, or 035) beyond an ISBN, ISSN, or OCLC number. Knowledge base vendors add these additional identifiers to keep track of the records within their own databases.

Blended Knowledge Management: ERMSs, Link Resolvers, and E-journal A–Z Lists

An ERMS is powered by a knowledge base and is used to capture both electronic holdings and other e-resource relevant acquisitions data. While librarians do not have the ability to directly modify the metadata contained within a knowledge base, they can use the ERMS to indicate which collections, packages, or individual resources their library subscribes to and the appropriate coverage dates for each one. For instance, a knowledge base may contain a collection of front-file e-journals available for subscription from a publisher. A library may subscribe to only one of these journals, and only from the year 2015, which is when the library first began its subscription. Through the ERMS, a librarian can select (or track or activate) the single journal title from the collection and change its coverage dates to 2015–present in order to accurately represent the available access. The ERMS can also control other aspects of access and display, such as whether to include a proxy prefix for titles or collections and the ability to include descriptions of access restrictions, such as seat or usage limitations. In other words, the knowledge base provides a reservoir of metadata from which a library can draw, but it is through an ERMS that the library indicates which metadata is relevant and adds additional information specific to the library's situation. Because edits cannot be made to the knowledge base itself but can be made to library selections, such as holdings and coverage dates, this knowledge management system has blended control.

Access disruptions originating from an ERMS, therefore, can be caused either by faulty metadata in the knowledge base, the symptoms of which we covered earlier, or from erroneously chosen holdings populated by a librarian. This could include such things as the following:

- incorrectly selected titles
- incorrect coverage dates
- missing proxy prefix
- erroneously added proxy prefix

These issues can result in patrons encountering paywalls and proxy error messages or being unable to find accessible content within the library's discovery service.

Many ERMSs are sold with link resolver functionality, but link resolvers can also be sold as stand-alone products or in conjunction with other access tools, such as e-journal A–Z lists. Like ERMSs, link resolvers consist of a knowledge base containing e-resource and linking data and an administrative interface through which a library may select its holdings. These holdings are then used to populate access tools, such as e-journal A–Z lists and discovery services. As a result, access issues are caused by either faulty metadata within the knowledge base or incorrect holdings chosen via the administrative interface. Symptoms would also be identical to those experienced by both a knowledge base and an ERMS, including broken or misdirecting links, paywalls, proxy error messages, and missing or erroneously included content.

Discovery Services

Discovery services are unique in that they utilize many of the access chain components we have discussed thus far in a single, unified search system. As detailed in figure 4.1, this could include knowledge bases, ERMSs, link resolvers, and central indexes as well as other components, such as APIs, institutional repositories, or an ILS. The access issues and related symptoms we have mentioned thus far in this chapter are all applicable in a discovery service environment and can be further complicated depending on the features and settings available to the discovery service itself. These features and settings often deal with promoting certain resources to the top of search results and may be marketed as Resource Recommender, Best Bets, or Topic Explorer. For instance, some libraries choose to make their research guides or database A–Z list entries discoverable via the discovery service. Therefore, it is essential to understand which components feed into the discovery system to better answer the question "Where is this metadata coming from?" Common symptoms in a discovery service environment could include the following:

- broken or misdirecting links
- hitting a paywall on the vendor platform
- not being prompted for authentication or proxy error messages

Library-Controlled Components: Common Issues and Symptoms

Outside of an online catalog, a library may employ several other access tools that fall primarily within their sphere of control, including a library website, database A–Z lists, and research guides. These access tools tend to be more self-contained, relying on librarians to add and manage their contents, rather than on metadata fed from third-party providers. We next cover the common causes and symptoms of issues originating in these access tools as well as discuss proxy servers and their configuration files, which are often maintained by library personnel.

A library's attitude toward adding access points to resources on the library website will vary based on the institution's philosophy and practices. Many libraries choose to use their websites to point to other access tools, such as their discovery services or database A–Z lists, rather than embedding hyperlinks to individual resources. However, this is not always the case. Furthermore, e-resource trouble-shooters may be the first to receive notice of other issues with the library website, such as embedded search bar widgets not loading or working properly. There-fore, understanding how the library website fits into the library's access chain and how that chain could break down is important. Potential causes of library website issues include the website server being offline, the library URL changing, outdated or incorrect hyperlinks, missing proxy prefixes, incorrect web script-ing, and incorrectly embedded widgets. Symptoms typically include 404 errors, patrons being unable to load the website, broken links, missing or unnecessary prompts for authentication, and embedded discovery search bars not loading or responding. These symptoms will likely be isolated to the website itself and will not extend to other access tools.

Database A–Z lists are typically created and maintained manually by librarians and, as a result, are prone to human error. Access disruptions originating from these lists often involve incorrectly entered data or data that is outdated. Com-mon examples include incorrect or outdated URLs, URLs missing proxy prefixes, missing entries for subscribed databases, or entries that have not been removed for canceled or unsubscribed databases. These issues generally result in broken links, not being prompted for authentication, or hitting a paywall on the vendor platform.

Just like with database A–Z lists, research guides are typically maintained manually by librarians, and access disruptions that originate from them are the result of missing or incorrect data. For instance, the URLs may be outdated or erroneously entered, be missing proxy prefixes, or may link to resources to which the library no longer subscribes or has access. Symptoms for these issues are mostly identical to the database A–Z list, including broken links, not being prompted for authentication, or hitting a paywall on the vendor platform. There-fore, it is essential to know where the patron encountered the access issue in order to identify where to go to correct it.

Proxy servers can be either locally hosted by the library or remotely hosted by a vendor or by an outside entity, such as a consortium. Depending on where the proxy server is hosted, your institution may not be able to make direct edits to the server or its configuration files. Like all servers, proxy servers can expe-rience downtime or lapses in access as a result of technical issues; however, for this chapter, we want to focus specifically on the configuration files. You will recall from chapter 2 that a proxy requires the maintenance of several config-uration files in order to function, including one that contains the URLs, hosts, and domains of the e-resources licensed for IP address authentication and access. These URLs, hosts, and domains are grouped together based on vendor platform into entries called stanzas and need to be frequently updated to keep pace with changes to the platform. Access issues originating within this configuration file are generally caused by missing, erroneous, or incomplete stanzas and will result in patrons being confronted with a proxy error message (these can be customized and so vary from institution to institution) or being forced to authenticate for open or free resources.

> **Troubleshooting Tip: Verifying If a Website Is Down**
>
> Did you know that there are several different websites that you can visit to verify if a given web page is down for just your PC (personal computer) or for everyone? The following websites allow you to plug in a URL to see how many users are affected by a vendor's potential downtime:
>
> - https://downforeveryoneorjustme.com/
> - https://www.isitdownrightnow.com/

Vendor-Controlled Components: Common Issues and Symptoms

Access issues originating from a vendor platform fall into two categories: technology issues with the platform itself, such as the server being offline or the platform relying on old or obsolete technology, and deliberate denials of access by the vendor, usually due to a belief that the library no longer has rights to access the content. For technology issues, the symptoms are what you might expect to find with any website, such as slow loading times, error messages, and pages, scripts, or images not displaying correctly. These symptoms are reproducible and can be very widespread, affecting not just your library and patrons but also libraries and patrons from across the vendor's consumer base. They also require action on the part of the vendor to be resolved. (The only gray area here may be when a platform requires a specific browser version to display correctly; yes, the issue can be resolved by the patron switching to the correct browser version, but if a platform runs on only a version of Internet Explorer that Microsoft stopped supporting years ago, is it not the vendor, rather than the patron, who should take action to fix things?)

Fortunately, these platform issues are relatively rare and, issues with obsolete web technology aside, tend to be addressed quickly by the vendor. Instead, troubleshooters are much more likely to encounter deliberate denials of access. Acquisitions issues, such as missed invoices or incorrectly applied payments, are the most frequent reasons a vendor would revoke access, but issues with content migration, excessive or suspicious usage and download activity (e.g., unauthorized scripting or text and data mining), and vendors updating their own platforms or customer data sets can also cause deliberate access denials.

Tracking Down the Cause

While reading through the lists of symptoms caused by dysfunctions within the various access chain components, you may have noticed significant overlap. Paywalls, for instance, feature prominently, as do broken or misdirecting links. So how does a troubleshooter go about determining where the cause actually lies?

Troubleshooters can employ a range of methods for tracking down the cause of a problem. These are some of the most common:

> *Re-creation:* Using this method, the troubleshooter isolates the cause of the issue by finding a procedure (sequence of steps or events) that consistently induces the symptoms/failure to occur.
>
> *Elimination:* Using this method, the troubleshooter isolates the cause of the issue by systematically testing and eliminating possible causes.
>
> *Backtracking:* Using this method, the troubleshooter isolates the cause of the issue by starting at the point of system failure and reasoning backward, testing each possible cause along the way (Gugerty 2007).
>
> *Half-splitting:* Using this method, the troubleshooter divides the system into portions and checks each portion for symptoms of the issue; this procedure is repeated in the portion where the symptoms occur (by again dividing and testing each half) until the cause of the issue has been isolated.

We have discussed re-creation and elimination already. Re-creation is perhaps the most widely employed and talked about method for e-resource troubleshooting. In their book *The ABCs of ERM*, Jessica Zellers, Tina M. Adams, and Katherine Hill (2018) list it as the first step in their four-part troubleshooting process, and also one that frontline staff should be trained to do before transferring problems to the "specialists" (158). We agree. By attempting to replicate an issue, the troubleshooter gains essential contextual information that verbal or written descriptions simply cannot provide. Often, this information is enough to pinpoint the cause of the access issue without the need for additional testing or investigation. However, even if additional testing is necessary, knowing whether an issue can be reproduced gives vital clues as to its nature and origin.

Elimination is another method frequently discussed in the library literature—although usually without naming it as such. The suggested strategies usually entail testing certain components, such as browsers, caches/cookies, or devices, by replacing or removing them from the access chain to see if the issue reappears. For instance, Jill Emery, Graham Stone, and Peter McCracken (2020) developed a browser rubric to systematically test popular browsers on Macs and PCs from both on and off campus (103). By diligently testing each combination, a troubleshooter can gain a comprehensive view of which factors—browser, device, and/or location—contribute to the appearance of the access failure.

Both re-creation and elimination are extremely useful in isolation; however, they alone cannot solve every issue. Sometimes, they will need to be used in conjunction with other troubleshooting methods to pinpoint the cause of an access disruption. Consider this example: a troubleshooter receives a problem report from a professor who cannot access an e-resource from within the learning management system (LMS). Through the troubleshooting interview, the troubleshooter learns that the professor had embedded one of the library's research guides within a course page, but when the professor clicked on the link to a database included in the guide, he received a 404 error message. Presuming the troubleshooter has access to the course page, the troubleshooter would first attempt to replicate the issue by navigating to the embedded guide and clicking the link. (Alternatively, the troubleshooter could navigate directly to the research guide from the library website to test the link there.) The troubleshooter receives the same 404 error message. After taking a closer look at the link, the troubleshooter discovers it is a friendly URL originating from the library's database A–Z list. The troubleshooter then navigates to the database A–Z list and tests that link. It, too, produces a 404 error message. Logging in to the backend of the A–Z list, the troubleshooter compares the entry's URL (the one masked by the friendly URL) to that currently being used on the database's homepage. The URLs are different. The troubleshooter updates the database entry to use the current homepage URL, which resolves the issue and allows the professor to access the database from within the LMS.

While re-creating the issue was an essential first step in diagnosis, replication alone was insufficient to pinpoint the cause. Because the URL of the link was passed through three access tools (database A–Z list to research guide to LMS course page) as well as hidden behind a friendly URL, simply finding and testing the link revealed very little as to why it was broken. Instead, the troubleshooter needed to follow the data back to its original source, testing along the way. This process of moving from LMS to research guide to database A–Z list is a technique called *backtracking*. This technique is most useful when trying to trace the origins of faulty metadata.

Half-splitting (also called *chunking* or the *divide-and-conquer method*) is another useful strategy for isolating the cause of an access issue. Using this method, the troubleshooter divides a system into segments (traditionally, into halves, thus the term *half-splitting*) and tests each segment for signs of the problem, repeating the process of dividing and testing until the faulty component is identified. Half-splitting is most effective when the troubleshooter is uncertain which area of the access chain an issue is originating from and wants to systematically test each portion, rather than randomly testing or eliminating components. For instance, let's imagine a troubleshooter is trying to determine why an off-campus patron is receiving a timeout error message when accessing an e-resource via the library's e-journal A–Z list. The troubleshooter could mentally divide the access chain into two halves: the patron-controlled components and authentication in one half and the e-journal A–Z list and vendor platform in another. To test the first half, the troubleshooter could provide the patron with a proxied link to a test e-resource—one the troubleshooter knows works correctly—and ask the patron to attempt to access the content. To test the second half, the troubleshooter navigates to the faulty e-journal within the A–Z list and attempts to access it first-hand. The troubleshooter is successfully able to view the journal on the vendor platform, but the patron reports that using the test link caused the timeout error message to appear.

Because the issue appeared again for the patron but not the troubleshooter, the next step would be to divide the first segment into its distinct pieces to test authentication and the patron-controlled components separately. To test the authentication, the troubleshooter could ask the patron to attempt to access an e-resource using the WAYF menu on an SSO-enabled vendor platform. This bypasses the proxy server entirely, while allowing the patron to use the same device, browser, and network connection as before. To test the device, browser, and network connection, the troubleshooter could first ask whether the patron has experienced connection issues, such as slow load times, while using non library web resources. The troubleshooter may also have the patron assess personal connection speed using a free online tool. However, the troubleshooter would likely want to wait for the results of the WAYF test before diving too far into such tests.

The patron reports being able to access the content using the WAYF menu and having no connection issues while browsing the web. This implies that some negative interaction with the proxy server (i.e., authentication) is at fault. Based on experience, the troubleshooter knows that browser cookies often interact negatively with the proxy server, so the troubleshooter would likely ask the patron to clear the cache and cookies as well as browsing history or attempt to use another browser entirely to see if either resolves the issue. If the issue persists or if more patrons report similar errors, the troubleshooter may want to consult with the staff who manage the proxy server in order to come to a satisfactory resolution, such as modifying the configurations or updating the server software.

Again, in this example, re-creation by itself was of limited value to the troubleshooter. Because the issue appeared for the patron but not the troubleshooter, it was difficult for the troubleshooter to gauge which components were contributing to the issue and which were extraneous. Similarly, while elimination may have eventually isolated the cause of the error, testing individual components in a sequential order—or, worse, jumping between components randomly or whenever inspiration strikes—is inefficient and can lead to frustration as time drags on. By chunking the access chain into segments and systematically testing each one, the troubleshooter was able to quickly home in on the culprit.

In addition to utilizing these general troubleshooting methods, troubleshooters often need information beyond that which can be gleaned from the access chain to determine the cause of an issue. Let's imagine that a troubleshooter receives a problem report from an internal reporter who is encountering a paywall when attempting to access an article while on campus. Paywalls can have several different causes, including issues with authentication, incorrect holdings, or the vendor platform itself, such as revoked access rights. Because the paywall was encountered while on campus, it is unlikely that authentication is the issue; however, just by looking at the access chain, it is impossible for the troubleshooter to know whether incorrect holdings or an issue on the vendor platform is to blame. To make this determination, the troubleshooter would first need to discover whether the library should have access to the material.

Acquisitions records are a natural first place to look. If the e-journal in question has a current order record and invoice payment, the question is answered: the holdings are accurate and the vendor needs to be contacted about the issue on its site. However, the absence of an acquisitions record does not necessarily mean that the holdings are incorrect, particularly if the resource was purchased or subscribed to as part of a larger package or included in a specialized agreement, like an evidence-based acquisition (EBA) plan. In these instances, the troubleshooter would need to dig further to find supporting documentation in the form of title lists or purchase notes. This may involve actions like reading the license or logging in to the vendor's administration portal to download a spreadsheet of the library's access entitlements.

Beyond holdings and acquisitions information, a troubleshooter may need to reference outside sources of information for items like publisher transfers, discontinuations, newly published titles, or title changes. Information sources troubleshooters may wish to consult include the following:

- OCLC
- Ulrich's Periodicals Directory
- Journal Transfer Notification Database
- library's order and invoice records
- library's subscription agent portal
- vendor's administration portal
- individual publisher websites
- license

Jump-Start Your Diagnosis

Not sure where to start? Here is our cheat sheet for diagnosing common issues:

- If you cannot reproduce the issue, have the reporter clear the cache and cookies and/or try a different browser.
- If you encounter a paywall while on campus, first check to see if the payment is up-to-date and includes the resource in question.
- If you encounter a paywall only while off campus, look more closely at authentication.
- If you encounter a broken or misdirecting link, first check to see if the content is accessible on the platform by navigating to it via an alternative route.
    - » If it is, the linking mechanism (metadata, URL, or link resolver) is likely at fault.
    - » If it is not (i.e., there is a paywall), check your acquisitions information.
    - » If the content is not on the platform at all, check to see if it has changed vendors or been discontinued.

Define the Scope

Most access issues are reported in isolation. A patron cannot access a particular article, book, or video and so reaches out for help, satisfied once the content is available again. As a result, troubleshooters also tend to diagnose issues in isolation, focusing only on restoring access to that singular article, book, or video. However, given the interconnectedness of library systems and the way libraries acquire their electronic resources, increasingly choosing subscriptions, packages, and plans over hand-selected purchases, access issues frequently affect more than just the resource or access tool that was reported.

Let's return to the example of the broken database link in the LMS course page. The troubleshooter traced the cause of the issue to an outdated URL in the library's database A–Z list, but many libraries also choose to catalog their databases in their ILSs so they appear within their online catalogs or discovery services. If this is the case, is it possible the URL contained in the catalog record is also incorrect? Or imagine that a troubleshooter discovers a paywall blocking access to an e-book the library purchased as part of a front-list package. If the vendor is denying the library access to this e-book, is it possible the vendor is also denying access to the other front-list titles? To fully grasp the breadth of the issue, therefore, it is important for the troubleshooter to ask these questions:

- How was this resource acquired?
- How is the resource made discoverable (e.g., discovery service, A–Z list, etc.)?
- What other resources might be affected?
- What other access tools might be affected?
- Has a similar issue been reported recently?

Because investigating scope can be a time-consuming prospect, troubleshooters will need to use their judgment when deciding when and how much time to invest in identifying larger issues.

Troubleshooting Tip: Are You Stuck?

Do not feel bad if you get stuck. We have all been there. If you are unable to move further with the methodologies that we have mentioned, here are some suggestions to help you gain traction:

E-mail the vendor: Ask the vendor to work with you to diagnose and resolve an issue; plenty of vendors have dedicated support specialists for this express purpose.

Check the resource's FAQs or support portal documentation: Many vendors document how best to use their products.

Post a question on an electronic discussion list: Some access tools have electronic discussion lists devoted to their products; alternatively, e-resource issues are frequently discussed on various professional library electronic discussion lists.

Consult a peer: A librarian at another institution may have similar access tools or e-resources and be able to help.

Example Scenarios

SCENARIO 1

In the previous chapter, a troubleshooter received a problem report from a graduate student about encountering broken links in the library's discovery service when attempting to access an article in the *Journal of Biology*. After examining the situation, the troubleshooter discovered that the two links displayed on the discovery record—one for a back-file journal package and one for a science journal package from the same vendor—resulted in the same "No results found" message on the vendor platform when clicked. Fortunately, the troubleshooter was able to navigate to the desired article via the library's e-journal A–Z list and provide it to the student, thus solving the patron-focused problem. However, the links on the discovery record are still broken. The troubleshooter now aims to figure out why.

Based on the initial investigation and the symptoms being displayed, the troubleshooter is already able to narrow down the possible causes of this issue. For example, the issue is likely unrelated to any patron-controlled components (device, browser, internet connection, etc.) because the issue was reproducible. The error message itself—"No results found"—also suggests that the problem is not with a device or browser, whose error messages tend to be about connection issues or content not loading properly. However, if the troubleshooter wants to verify this fact, the troubleshooter could try eliminating these components as possible causes by testing different browsers, trying the browser in incognito mode, or testing the links from a different device.

The problem is also unlikely to be with the vendor platform. Because the troubleshooter was able to retrieve the article via an alternative route, the troubleshooter knows the article is available and accessible. The article simply was not linked to properly. This narrows down the components to those contributing to the linking functions in the discovery service, namely, the knowledge base, link resolver, and the central index. As a result, the troubleshooter suspects that there is an issue with how the article's metadata is interacting with the OpenURL resolver.

To confirm this suspicion, the troubleshooter reexamines the article citation on the discovery service record and compares it to the article's citation on the vendor platform. The troubleshooter spots an inaccuracy: the discovery record lists the article as appearing in volume 6 of the journal; however, the article actually appears in volume 63. This is likely what is causing the link to fail. Furthermore, the troubleshooter knows that article metadata comes from the central index, as opposed to a knowledge base, which means the troubleshooter has pinpointed the issue to this component.

SCENARIO 2

In the previous chapter, a troubleshooter engaged in a chat with a student who could not access an article in the *Journal of Education*. Through the troubleshooting interview, the troubleshooter learned that the student had attempted to access the article through the library's discovery service while at home but had encountered a paywall on the vendor platform. The troubleshooter investigated the situation by finding the discovery record and trying the links firsthand. Despite being on campus, the troubleshooter also encountered the paywall on the vendor platform. Because the troubleshooter was unable to provide immediate access to the content and the patron had indicated that she needed the article as soon as possible, the troubleshooter referred her to interlibrary loan, thus solving the patron-focused problem. However, the article remains inaccessible. The troubleshooter next aims to find out why.

The troubleshooter is able to eliminate the patron-controlled components as likely origination points of the problem. This is because the issue was reproducible, having been experienced by both the problem reporter and the troubleshooter. Similarly, the troubleshooter is able to eliminate the knowledge base and central index from consideration because these components are used primarily for discoverability and linking, both of which seem to be working properly. Instead, paywalls tend to be the result of issues with authentication, the electronic holdings in a knowledge management system (e.g., ERMS or LSP), or the vendor platform. To help narrow it down, the troubleshooter decides to investigate the scope of the issue. The troubleshooter checks to see if other articles within the journal are accessible—they are not—and then checks to see if another subscribed journal on the vendor platform is accessible—it is. Because the issue is isolated to just the *Journal of Education*, it is unlikely that faulty authentication is the cause of the issue. Instead, the most likely culprits are incorrect holdings within the knowledge management system (i.e., the library does not actually subscribe to the journal) or a deliberate denial of access on the vendor platform (i.e., access being cut due to nonpayment or miscommunication).

The troubleshooter's next step is to determine if the library should have access to the e-journal. The troubleshooter could do this in a couple ways, including reaching out to a library acquisitions staff member or the vendor to ask about the journal's subscription status. Because the troubleshooter is able to access the library's acquisitions records, the troubleshooter decides to check this firsthand. Within the LSP, the troubleshooter finds an order record for an education journal package from the same publisher that offers the *Journal of Education*. The journal package is managed by the library's subscription agent, so the troubleshooter logs on to the subscription agent's portal to try to find a title list for the package. Upon finding the title list, the troubleshooter verifies that the library does not have access to the *Journal of Education*.

SCENARIO 3

In the previous chapter, a troubleshooter received an e-mail from a faculty professor who was unable to view the film *Rashomon*, which the professor wanted to show in an upcoming class. The troubleshooter learned that the professor had been attempting to access the film from off campus during the weekend and had encountered a message that said the library was not subscribed to the film. The troubleshooter investigated the situation by navigating to the resource while on campus and encountered the same paywall as the professor. Because the film was not available via another video platform, the troubleshooter was unable to provide immediate access to the resource. This means the patron-focused problem remains unsolved until the technology-focused issue is resolved.

As with the previous scenario, the troubleshooter is able to narrow down the cause as an issue with authentication, the electronic holdings in a knowledge management system, or the vendor platform. The troubleshooter can further refine this by determining the scope of the issue. The troubleshooter tests other videos on the platform and is able to view and play them, which indicates the issue likely lies either with the holdings in the knowledge management system or with a deliberate denial of access on the vendor platform.

The troubleshooter's next step is to determine if the library should have access to the streaming video. Like before, the troubleshooter checks the acquisitions records in the LSP to verify if the video in question is included on an access title list and if the library's payment is up-to-date. The troubleshooter wants to make sure that the library should have access to this particular streaming video and did not load its MARC record by accident. Upon examining the acquisitions records, the troubleshooter sees that the video was recently purchased due to high usage.

Conclusion

Diagnosing can be a lengthy and recursive process with troubleshooters retracing their steps when a given line of thought proves unfruitful. To aid in these difficulties, it can be very helpful for troubleshooters to consider both where this metadata is coming from and who controls the metadata associated with a given problem report. After reviewing these facets of the issue, troubleshooters can then move on to analyzing the problem report's access chain and considering its common points of failure. With this base knowledge, they can begin to determine why the access issue occurred based on the evidence presented and formulate possible solutions. The symptoms of the common issues prevalent in different access tools often overlap, and it can sometimes be helpful to reflect on problem reports from this angle in order to more effectively diagnose an issue. If after defining the scope of an issue and attempting to use various methods for tracking down the cause of a problem, such as elimination or half-splitting, troubleshooters still struggle to generate solutions, they can consult both local and third-party information sources to jump-start their brainstorming.

ADDITIONAL READINGS AND RESOURCES

Browning, Sommer. 2015. "Data, Data, Everywhere, nor Any Time to Think: DIY Analysis of E-resource Access Problems." *Journal of Electronic Resources Librarianship* 27 (1): 26–34. doi:10.1080/1941126X.2015.999521.

Calarco, Pascal, Lettie Conrad, Rachel Kessler, and Michael Vandenburg. 2014. "Metadata Challenges in Library Discovery Systems." In *Proceedings of the Charleston Library Conference*, 533–540. Purdue University, Purdue e-Pubs. http://dx.doi.org/10.5703/1288284315642.

Graham, Tess, and Nate Hosburgh. 2014. "A User-Centered Approach to Addressing Issues of Discoverability and Access." *Serials Librarian* 67 (1): 48–51.

Rodriguez, Michael, Joel Tonyan, and Robert T. Wilson. 2018. "Tools and Techniques for Troubleshooting Remote Access." *Journal of Electronic Resources Librarianship* 30 (3): 171–78. doi:10.1080/1941126X.2018.1494095.

Wilson, Kristen. 2016. "The Knowledge Base at the Center of the Universe." *Library Technology Reports* 52 (6): 1–35.

REFERENCES

Emery, Jill, Graham Stone, and Peter McCracken. 2020. "Troubleshooting." In *Techniques for Electronic Resource Management: TERMS and the Transition to Open*, 91–116. Chicago: ALA Editions.

Gugerty, Leo. 2007. "Cognitive Components of Troubleshooting Strategies." *Thinking and Reasoning* 13 (2): 134–63. doi:10.1080/13546780600750641.

Zellers, Jessica, Tina M. Adams, and Katherine Hill. 2018. "I Think the Internet Broke." In *The ABCs of ERM: Demystifying Resource Management for Public and Academic Librarians*, 154–68. Santa Barbara, CA: Libraries Unlimited.

5

Resolving Access Issues

Once a troubleshooter has uncovered the probable cause of an access issue, it is time to work toward a resolution. This will involve the last four stages of the seven-stage troubleshooting process discussed in chapter 1, namely:

4. Consider the possible solutions.
5. Implement the solution.
6. Review the results.
7. Communicate and document the resolution.

Generating Solutions

Solutions to many technology-focused problems are straightforward: if a troubleshooter discovers an outdated link in a database A–Z list, the solution is to replace it; if a MARC record was erroneously loaded into the catalog, the solution is to remove it. However, troubleshooters may run into issues for which the solution is not immediately obvious or multiple solutions are possible. In these cases, it is necessary for the troubleshooter to generate a list of possible solutions and consider the benefits and drawbacks of implementing one solution over another.

When brainstorming potential solutions, troubleshooters should begin by identifying the component(s) causing the access issue and under whose control it falls: patron, library, vendor, or a blend. Most solutions will involve modifying this component, so knowing who has the ability to effect change within it is essential. Additionally, troubleshooters should consider the components that surround and interact with the faulty one, paying particular attention to the flow of data within the access chains utilizing them. Doing so can not only help troubleshooters uncover solutions they might not otherwise have considered but also allow them to spot any unintended ripple effects.

For example, let's imagine that a troubleshooter receives a problem report about a link to an e-journal leading to a "Page not found" error message on the vendor platform. Upon investigating the issue, the troubleshooter discovers that the e-journal was part of an aggregator collection to which the library subscribed but the title had changed publishers several months ago, leading the vendor to drop the title from its platform. Because the library no longer has access to the content through the aggregator collection, the troubleshooter needs to remove the e-journal from discovery. First, the troubleshooter identifies which components are responsible for providing the erroneous access. In this case, the e-journal was activated as part of a collection from the library's ERMS knowledge base. The ERMS has its control split between the vendor, who has the ability to edit the knowledge base itself, and the library, who has the ability to modify which knowledge base titles and collections are activated.

What solutions are available to the troubleshooter? Because the e-journal left an aggregator collection, the library could notify the ERMS vendor to remove the title from the collection in the knowledge base. Once the knowledge base is corrected, the e-journal would be deleted automatically from the library's holdings as part of a future update. Alternatively, the troubleshooter could manually deactivate the title from the collection. This would not modify the knowledge base itself but would remove the title from the library's holdings. However, when thinking about how the knowledge base interacts with the library's holdings in the ERMS, the troubleshooter discovers an unintended consequence: libraries that selectively activate titles within a collection (as opposed to activating them all) no longer have new titles automatically activated as they are added to the collection in the knowledge base. This means if the faulty title is deactivated by the troubleshooter, the library would need to manually maintain the collection going forward.

These types of pitfalls are increasingly common as library systems become more tightly coupled. Actions taken to solve one problem inadvertently produce another. Therefore, it is important for troubleshooters to consider the standards and best practices for the systems in which they are working, especially in regard to acquisitions, cataloging, and discoverability. Troubleshooters should aim not just to alleviate the symptoms but to put the system as close to its ideal state as possible.

Troubleshooting Tip: Generating Solutions

- What component(s) is causing the access issue and why?
- Who has the ability to effect change within the component(s)?
- What other components interact with the faulty one(s)?
- Can a change in another component cause a similar effect?
- How does the data flow within the affected access chain(s)? Will there be any unintended consequences?

Troubleshooting Tip: Sources to Consult for Solutions

- Ask the vendor.
- Read product documentation.
- Post a question to an electronic discussion list or search its archive.
- Ask a peer.
- Conduct an internet search.

Intermediary Actions and Stopgap Solutions

Troubleshooters should consider if any intermediary actions or stopgap solutions are necessary while awaiting the primary resolution to an access issue. These actions are used to alleviate some of the frustration and confusion patrons feel while a resource is unavailable or lacking other functionality for an extended period of time.

For example, imagine there is a stanza missing from an EZproxy configuration file that is resulting in a proxy error message when accessing a database. If the proxy server is hosted remotely, such as by a consortium or vendor, the troubleshooter would need to submit a request for the change that may take some time to be processed. This means, depending on the responsiveness of the vendor, the troubleshooter may want to consider additional actions, such as hiding the database record, removing the proxy from the link so it is accessible only on campus, or adding a note about the issue to the database A–Z list while it is being resolved.

Just as troubleshooters will often find themselves weighing one solution against another, intermediary stopgap measures need to be weighed against potential consequences. Review again the questions that we mentioned for how to generate solutions, and consider the following intermediary actions and stopgap measures:

- Temporarily suppress the faulty record.
- Place a note about the issue on the resource record.

- Ask interlibrary loan staff to fill requests while the e-resource is unavailable.
- Remove the EZproxy prefix.
- Contact the vendor to turn on e-resource access in the meantime.

When communicating with patrons before a solution can be fully implemented, the troubleshooter should attempt to give an estimated time for resolution to the patron and also attempt to manage any expectations the patron may have. As Susan Davis and colleagues (2012) eloquently state:

> Managing expectations of turnaround time is important as well, especially if the patron is a particularly vocal member of the community (for instance, a prestigious faculty member). Public relations skills are put to use to create realistic expectations and also being transparent about sharing information is important. (31)

For example, if a patron mentions having a research paper that is due in a few days and the troubleshooter suspects that the desired e-resource will not be available by the patron's deadline, the troubleshooter should proactively mention this to the patron and provide the patron with assistance either in locating other suitable sources or in contacting a library coworker who can further assist the patron.

Evaluating Solutions

When multiple solutions to a single issue are available, they are often not equal in terms of the time and effort required to implement them nor in their ramifications. In most cases, these differences make the best path forward self-evident—the troubleshooter need only choose the fastest, most efficient, or least negative option. However, there may be instances when the correct decision is not as obvious and troubleshooters will need to evaluate the options to determine which course of action is best for their libraries.

Consider this example: a troubleshooter discovers that some (but not all) direct links to articles from a full-text database are broken in the library's discovery service. These direct links are provided via the discovery service's central index and are therefore under the vendor's control. The troubleshooter could take several different courses of action to resolve this issue. Because the central index can be modified by only the discovery service vendor, the troubleshooter could simply report the issue to the vendor and wait for the vendor to resolve it. This solution is relatively easy for the troubleshooter but may prove to be a lengthy process, depending on the response time of the vendor. In the meantime, the broken links would remain discoverable, inconveniencing patrons.

Alternatively, the troubleshooter could also choose to deactivate the full-text database within the central index. Doing so would remove all the article-level records for that database, including both those with the faulty links and those that are linking correctly. The benefit of this is twofold: first, the patrons would be less frustrated because they would not be encountering those broken links; and second, it would prevent additional problem reports from being submitted, allowing staff to address new issues rather than repeatedly responding to a known issue. By removing the records, however, the library is not only preventing patrons from discovering the content but also removing examples for the vendor to reference while working toward a resolution. Additionally, the troubleshooter would need to remember to reactivate the database within the central index once the vendor has fixed the issue.

There is no single right answer in this scenario. One library may value maintaining the content within the discovery service, preferring to assist patrons as they encounter issues rather than hide the problems from view; whereas another library may value the user experience of the discovery service over the content, choosing to hide from patrons content that may confuse or frustrate them. Which course of action the troubleshooter chooses will depend entirely on the library's values and the particular circumstances of the situation, such as the popularity of the resource, other avenues to the content's discoverability, and the staffing available to address ongoing reports of broken links.

Given the uniqueness of many troubleshooting situations, no list could fully encompass the potential factors to consider when weighing solutions. What is right for one library may not be tenable for another. However, a few questions do regularly appear in both the library science literature and the field of problem solving that, when answered, can help steer troubleshooters in the right direction:

- How easy or difficult is the solution to implement? What time and resources are required to enact it?
    - » Can it be implemented locally or will you need to ask for outside help?
    - » How much time and effort will it take? When can you expect to see results?
    - » Is the solution cost-effective?
    - » Will anyone need to learn new skills?

- How urgently is a solution needed? Does the issue need to be addressed immediately or can it become a back-burner project?
    - » How many people are affected by the problem?
    - » Is the content unique to the affected resource? Is it heavily used?
    - » Is the affected resource accessible through another access tool? What about interlibrary loan?

- How effective is the solution?
  - » Does it address the entire scope of the problem?
  - » Is it treating the underlying cause or just the symptoms? Is it likely the issue will reoccur?
  - » Will the solution require additional follow-up?

- What is the impact of the solution?
  - » What effects (positive and negative) will it have on patrons? Library staff? The larger community?
  - » How will it affect organizational morale?
  - » How will it affect public relations?

- Is it consistent with other actions taken by the library?
  - » Does the solution align with your library's strategic plan or goals
  - » Does the solution positively or negatively affect patron expectations?

When faced with tough decisions, troubleshooters should seek out additional feedback from others, including their manager, library leadership, and additional stakeholders. For example, troubleshooters should consult with their library coworkers who are familiar with the affected patron group or who may be shouldering additional work if a particular course of action is chosen. Doing so ensures the best possible decision is made for the library and its patrons and increases buy-in from those affected by the decision. We discuss making decisions in a collaborative team environment more in chapter 7.

Implementing the Solution

Once a solution has been chosen, it is time to put it into action. Depending on the components involved, this could mean troubleshooters implementing the solution themselves or working with another person, such as the patron, a library colleague, or a vendor representative, to implement it on their behalf.

Ideally, if troubleshooters are tasked with enacting the solution themselves, they will already have the prerequisite knowledge to make the adjustments within the necessary components. However, e-resources break in new and interesting ways all the time, and as a result, troubleshooters may run into issues for which they need to deploy a solution outside their current skill set. Just like with diagnosis and solution generation, troubleshooters can consult outside informational sources to augment their technical knowledge. For instance, they could consult an electronic discussion list archive for further information regarding their problem report or post a question to the list itself if a particular issue proves persistent and they think others libraries may also be affected. Additionally, troubleshooters could use a search engine to look up support documentation or how to complete a task, such as making an EZproxy stanza. Vendors of both access tools and e-resources sometimes have online support documentation available to their customers.

> **Troubleshooting Tip: Finding EZproxy Stanzas**
> Did you know that OCLC keeps a list of up-to-date database stanzas? If you are looking to add or replace an EZproxy stanza, start by checking the OCLC's website: https://help.oclc.org/Library_Management/EZproxy/Database_stanzas. In addition to OCLC, many vendors are able to provide stanzas for their products upon request. So, if you're struggling to make or modify a stanza, try e-mailing the vendor to get the vendor's input.

> **Troubleshooting Tip: Test Before Implementing a Solution**
> Did you know that some products have ways to test changes before they are implemented? For instance, Ex Libris's Alma LSP comes with a standard sandbox environment where the library can try out fixes to see if they will work or result in any unanticipated issues. This is especially helpful if you are uncertain what ramifications a change may have.

Issues originating within a patron-controlled component (device, browser, network connection, etc.) will require action by the patron to reach resolution. Troubleshooters need to provide clear, precise instructions for any steps the patron needs to complete. Remember that many patrons have only cursory knowledge of the library's technical systems and so may become confused or frustrated if troubleshooters use too much jargon or unfamiliar technical terms. If library jargon is unavoidable, be sure to provide explanations for terms the patron may not know and give the patron ample opportunity to ask for further direction or clarification. Troubleshooters may even want to supplement their written instructions with screenshots or screen recordings that visually show the patrons what to do.

To save themselves from constantly re-creating instructions, many libraries create ready-made documentation in the form of searchable web pages or research guides. This documentation covers resolutions to common issues, such as clearing caches and cookies, resetting organizational passwords, editing browser security settings, and downloading vendor-required software, like Adobe Digital Editions. Making these pages publicly available allows patrons to revisit the instructions in the future, in case they run into similar circumstances and want to try troubleshooting themselves. Here are two research guides to look at for inspiration:

- Shapiro Library at Southern New Hampshire University: https://libguides .snhu.edu/troubleshooting
- University of Texas Libraries at the University of Texas at Austin: https:// guides.lib.utexas.edu/ETS

We discuss more examples in chapter 7, and they are listed under the Additional Readings and Resources section there.

Issues originating within library- and vendor-controlled components may require troubleshooters to coordinate fixes among multiple entities, departments, and library colleagues. To solve an acquisitions payment issue, for instance, the troubleshooter may need to work with the acquisitions staff in the technical services department, the accountants in the library's business office, and a sales representative from the vendor. To remove an IP address block due to excessive downloading, the troubleshooter may need to involve the systems librarian, campus IT staff, and vendor support personnel. When enlisting the help of others to resolve an access issue, troubleshooters should remember to include the following in their request:

- a concise explanation of the problem and why it is occurring
- what actions the person needs to take and why
- how urgently the fix is needed
- any other relevant information discovered by the troubleshooter during investigation

Vendor support representatives may need additional information, particularly if they are unfamiliar with the library, its systems, and its history with the vendor. Relevant items to mention include the library's name, account number, and address as well as the troubleshooter's name, position, and contact information. The troubleshooter should also provide a succinct summary of what has been tried thus far to solve the issue and other information relevant to the situation, such as invoice numbers or payment dates. By proactively considering what the vendor may need to troubleshoot a given issue, a troubleshooter can help the vendor expedite a solution.

Although many support representatives are extremely knowledgeable and helpful, these positions experience frequent turnover, and as a result, troubleshooters should not assume that all support staff are fluent in how their own company's technology works or in how library technology works. If troubleshooters are having difficulties with a particular support representative, they should feel confident escalating their issue and requesting another support representative to work with after interactions with the original representative have proved unfruitful. Even if a vendor has been historically unresponsive to a library's requests for customer service, troubleshooters should still feel compelled to report issues to the vendor for the benefit of the vendor's other customers. Especially if a given issue concerns the library's central index or knowledge base, always reporting issues is the best proactive step to enact change for the greater good.

> **Troubleshooting Tip: Vendor Administration Portal**
> Did you know that many vendors provide their customers with administrative portals for their platforms? Administration portals are a great place to go if you are feeling stuck or are looking for additional information regarding the content provided on a specific platform. Although the content and functionality can vary, most administration portals contain information about the library's account number, sales or customer support representative, registered IP addresses, and titles lists, showing the library's subscriptions, purchases, and/or perpetual access. Vendors may also include notices about planned downtimes, renewal/expiration dates, and blocks on the account due to suspicious activity.

Reviewing Results

Once a solution has been implemented, troubleshooters should verify that the access issue has been successfully resolved. Generally, this can be accomplished by attempting to re-create the issue once more to see if it appears. However, even if the symptoms of the access issue have dissipated, troubleshooters may wish to check back periodically to review results and ensure that the solution has stuck. How often to review results is entirely dependent upon the problem reported and the vendors, e-resources, or access tools involved. Standard database features being reenabled, newly enabled access to paid content, EZproxy updates, and corrected article-level links are all instances when troubleshooters should review the results of the solution.

A large part of reviewing results is remaining cognizant if similar issues are reported soon after a solution has been implemented. For example, if a vendor updates its website architecture and notifies subscribers ahead of time, a library could probably proactively update its metadata for the vendor platform and not receive any problem reports regarding the issue. However, if all does not go as planned and the vendor continues to update its platform throughout the following week, the library's updates are no longer valid and a troubleshooter would need to review the new updates and check back to make sure the library's metadata for the vendor's platform is correct.

Out-of-the-Box Solutions for Big-Picture Issues

Some problem reports can lead to larger concerns regarding user experience. Troubleshooters can work with their coworkers on these issues in order to best meet their patrons' needs. Especially when problem reports are repeatedly received for the same issue, thinking outside of the box for innovative solutions to meet patron needs is recommended. For example, if a library was to receive a great number of reports about missing content that had erroneously been made discoverable, the library could choose to purchase or subscribe to the resource in question after so much need and interest had been demonstrated for it. This decision would require troubleshooters to provide enough information to collection development staff to make an informed decision. The conversation would likely begin as an informal suggestion and rely on the troubleshooters' initiative to mention the relevant information to their coworkers.

More common examples of potential collaboration would be updating access tool features with customizations specific to your library's patrons or e-resources. For example, you may want to add icons in your database A–Z list for resources that require the use of an account, a username/password, or specific browser to access them. Another common customization point is the button prevalent within many access tools and e-resources that allows patrons to discover full-text content by connecting them to the library's link resolver. Different libraries choose to label their buttons in various ways, from "Check for full text" to "Find full text." These types of decisions can often best be made by both public and technical services staff collaborating and striking a balance between what would be best for your library's patrons and what is technologically feasible within the settings of your library's access tools or e-resources. Public services staff can also be instrumental in patron education and managing their expectations as they incorporate the informed decisions and the reasoning behind them into their instruction sessions and day-to-day patron interactions.

Communication and Documentation

The final phase in the troubleshooting process is communicating and documenting the resolution. Communication involves both following up with the initial problem reporter to inform the patron of the resolution and sharing the results of the troubleshooting process with necessary stakeholders, such as public services staff or other members of the troubleshooting team.

Following up may look different depending on whether the initial problem reporter was internal or external to the library and if the patron-focused problem was resolved before the technology-focused one. Generally, it is best practice to follow up with all reporters once an issue has been fully resolved, regardless of the elapsed time. The message should briefly explain the outcome of the resolution, provide instructions on how (or whether) the content can be accessed going forward, and invite the reporter to contact the troubleshooter again if similar issues arise. However, there may be instances when following up with each reporter is not necessary or possible. In these cases, the troubleshooter may need to creatively prioritize which tickets to respond to and in what order.

Follow-up is mandatory and should be prioritized first for reporters waiting on a resolution to a patron-focused problem. With the remaining reporters, follow-up may be prioritized depending on the access issue involved, the level of interest they've expressed, or how vocal they are within the community. Usually after a troubleshooter's initial response to a reporter, which states that the issue will be attended to, the reporter will let the troubleshooter know if the troubleshooter should notify the reporter when the issue has been fixed. For example, a particularly prolific researcher may be more curious than other patrons about the inner workings of library technology because the researcher is more likely to encounter broken links and other e-resource issues while conducting research.

Aside from following up with problem reporters, troubleshooters may want to communicate and document resolutions more widely if doing so has value for the following:

- future troubleshooting
- e-resource management knowledge
- library coworkers who frequently work with patrons one-on-one
- other stakeholders who would be affected by information newly discovered from a problem report

The presence of any such value would require a troubleshooter to coordinate and communicate new information to various coworkers as necessary. For example, during the course of resolving a problem report, a troubleshooter may discover that a certain database works well with only one browser. The troubleshooter would want to disseminate this information both to the public services staff who regularly assist patrons and directly to the patrons themselves. The troubleshooter could opt to place a note next to the entry on the database A–Z list or include it on a library web page, such as for frequently asked questions (FAQs), so that future patrons do not encounter the same issue. Other examples include working with e-resource management staff when a troubleshooter verifies acquisitions information about a subscription or working with subject liaisons who provide instruction sessions to patrons on the best practices of working with certain e-resources.

In regard to future troubleshooting, a troubleshooter may need to document newly discovered information about an e-resource or its vendor. For example, a troubleshooter may discover that a professor's account for the library's art image database is limited to downloading 250 images per year. This information was not documented anywhere on the vendor website and was discovered only after multiple phone calls with the vendor's library relations representative, communication that was necessary to determine why the professor could no longer download images from the database. The troubleshooter would want to document this information for the benefit of future troubleshooters. The troubleshooter could store this information in acquisitions records, in the library's ERMS, in a nonpublic note on the e-resources catalog record, or elsewhere in shared troubleshooting documentation. Other troubleshooting items to document can include any relevant communication e-mails, stored in a centralized location, or previously undocumented, account-identifying information received from the vendor. The final step of documentation is to ensure that the problem report is closed out within a library's records or help ticket system. All necessary, smaller tasks that were generated by the problem report have been attended to, and the troubleshooter completes any other work that is required to consider the problem report as closed.

Triage

Not all access issues are urgent; however, when major or widespread access issues occur, effective communication and documentation are essential for bringing about a swift and satisfactory resolution. Most libraries have plans in place for emergency situations, whether it be power outages, technology failures, floods, or other natural disasters. We recommend having a similar plan in place for troubleshooting in case disaster strikes. By thinking through the response process ahead of time, troubleshooters can have a plan of action in place so that information and updates can be disseminated as quickly as possible to patrons, library coworkers, and other stakeholders.

Major access issues libraries have experienced in the past include a vendor cutting off access to a highly used database, campus IT changing entire IP ranges without notifying the library ahead of time, massive cloud-hosting server outages that affected multiple vendors and e-resources, and proxy servers going down for extended periods of time. These scenarios involve lengthy resolutions with a great amount of back-and-forth troubleshooting with third parties, and they often result in a massive amount of problem reports being submitted to a library. In these situations, troubleshooters move from troubleshooting to triage in that they are forced to assign degrees of urgency to tickets to determine their order of troubleshooting. No matter how well resourced a troubleshooting workflow is, it can be very difficult to properly triage a catastrophic or systemic issue. Major access issues require detailed plans:

- communication plan to all patrons, library coworkers, or other library stakeholders:
    - » What e-resources, vendors, or access tools are affected?
    - » What undesirable behavior is occurring?
    - » Are there any intermediary solutions?
    - » When is the issue expected to be resolved?

- communication plan to vendors:
    - » Identify your top ten vendors that are the most important to reestablish access with as soon as possible.
    - » After initial contact with a vendor, stay on top of the issue to ensure that progress toward resolution does not stall.
    - » Escalate the issue if necessary; seek out additional support from the third party.
    - » Explain the gravity of the situation if you feel that the third party is not in agreement with you concerning the urgency of the situation.

- additional customer service support:
    - » Create a predetermined message for troubleshooting staff to use when answering similar problem reports about the issue.
    - » If a high-profile patron is involved, collaborate with other library coworkers and keep them in the loop with updates so that the high-profile patron receives the level of customer service which that patron expects.

Much of successfully handling a major access issue comes down to communication. The quicker the issue can be made known to those affected via as many communication avenues as possible, the better. We recommend a combination of the following:

- announcement to library coworkers via e-mail (such as through an all-staff e-mail list)
- notices posted on the library website
- notices posted to the discovery service or A–Z lists
- depending on the resource and severity of the issue, announcement posted to the library's social media accounts

Any announcement regarding access issues should explain what issue is occurring, including the types of errors patrons may be encountering, as well as an assurance that you (or, in general, the library) are currently working to resolve it. As you work to resolve the issue with the vendor, IT department, and other relevant personnel, be sure to keep open the channels of communication to your library leadership and frontline staff. Let them know of any helpful updates and assure them that the issue is being taken seriously. Once the issue is resolved, make an announcement via the same channels and remove any notice banners you have placed on the website, A–Z lists, and discovery service. And, of course, ask staff to continue reporting any further issues they encounter.

Example Scenarios

SCENARIO 1

In the previous chapter, the troubleshooter investigated why a link in the discovery service to an article in the *Journal of Biology* was producing a "No results found" error message. The troubleshooter was able to reproduce the issue, which indicated that the patron-controlled components were not at fault, and was able to navigate to the article via an alternative route, suggesting that the issue lay within the components involved in discovery service linking functions, such as the knowledge base, link resolver, or central index. Upon comparing the metadata of the article's discovery record to that on the vendor platform, the troubleshooter uncovered an inconsistency: the discovery record lists the article as appearing in volume 6 of the journal; however, the article actually appears in volume 63. This means the error was caused by incorrect metadata coming from the discovery service's central index. Next, the troubleshooter sets out to fix the issue.

The troubleshooter first considers the faulty component and who has the ability to effect change within it. The central index is maintained by the discovery service's vendor, so to initiate a change to its metadata, the troubleshooter would need to submit a ticket to the vendor's support portal. The troubleshooter also considers the surrounding and dependent components and what solutions may be available through them, such as disabling the central index collection responsible for the metadata on the backend of the discovery service. However, the negative impact of this solution far outweighs the good. The troubleshooter decides the best course of action is to submit a ticket to the vendor and wait for the vendor to correct the metadata.

The troubleshooter submits a ticket to the discovery services vendor via its support portal, making sure to include the appropriate permalink to the faulty record and a detailed explanation of the issue and its cause. From past experience, the troubleshooter knows that tickets submitted to the support portal frequently take a long time to reach a resolution, and so the troubleshooter makes a to-do list item to follow up with the vendor in a month's time. Two weeks later, a support technician from the vendor responds to the ticket to indicate the issue has been escalated to the vendor's metadata team for further evaluation. The troubleshooter makes a note of this on the to-do list.

SCENARIO 2

In the previous chapter, the troubleshooter investigated why a student was encountering a paywall while trying to access an article in the *Journal of Education* via the library's discovery service. The troubleshooter was able to reproduce the issue, also encountering a paywall despite being located on campus. The troubleshooter was also not able to access the article via an alternative route. This implied that the vendor had cut access to the article on the platform. Upon investigating the scope of the issue, the troubleshooter discovered that all articles to the *Journal of Education* were inaccessible. The troubleshooter then verified via acquisition records and the library's subscription agent that the library does not currently subscribe to the journal. Next, the troubleshooter aims to fix the issue.

The troubleshooter first considers the component responsible for providing the erroneous holdings and who has the ability to effect change within it. The electronic holdings for this journal were provided via the e-resources module within the library's LSP. Fortunately, the troubleshooter has access to this module, so the troubleshooter can make direct modifications to the holdings without needing to e-mail another staff member. The troubleshooter logs in to the LSP, searches for the *Journal of Education*, and discovers it was activated as part of a larger publisher collection from the LSP's knowledge base. The troubleshooter also realizes that far too many e-journals have been tracked for the publisher in question. "All access" (all of the titles with the publisher) has been tracked instead of the partial access for which their library has actually paid. The troubleshooter then creates a to-do list item to use the discovered title list to retrack the library's titles in the LSP as soon as possible.

SCENARIO 3

In the previous chapter, the troubleshooter investigated why a professor was encountering a "Library not subscribed" message when attempting to access the film *Rashomon*. The troubleshooter was able to reproduce the issue, also encountering the message despite being located on campus. This implied that the vendor had cut access to the video on their platform. The troubleshooter then verified via acquisition records that the library had recently purchased the streaming video due to high usage and therefore should have access. Unfortunately, the troubleshooter was unable to provide the professor immediate access to the film via another source or access method, so the patron-focused problem remains unsolved. The troubleshooter next aims to restore access.

First, the troubleshooter considers who has the ability to restore access to the film on the vendor platform. For some platforms, the library activates newly acquired e-resources via an entitlements token provided in an e-mail from the vendor. This platform does not work this way. Instead, access can be added or removed by only the vendor itself. However, the troubleshooter has multiple ways to contact the vendor, including e-mailing the sales representative or filling out a general support form on the vendor's website. From past experience, the troubleshooter knows that the sales representative is extremely responsive to e-mail requests and so decides to contact that person directly in the hopes of a speedy resolution.

The troubleshooter makes note of the invoice number and payment date from the acquisitions record before e-mailing the sales representative:

> To: <salesrep@video.vendor.edu>
> From: <troubleshooting@email.university.edu>
> Subject: Missing Access to Rashomon
>
> Hello,
> I am Troubleshooter with University Library; our account # is 555. We currently do not have access to the video *Rashomon*. Our records show that payment was processed 11/1/19. Please let me know what further information I can provide to reinstate access to the video.
>
> Sincerely,
> Troubleshooter
> Troubleshooter Job Title
> Library Name
> Address
> Phone Number

Upon checking its accounts and records, the vendor agrees with the troubleshooter and turns the library's access back on. The troubleshooter notifies the faculty member that the library's access to the video has been restored.

To: <lehane@email.university.edu>
From: <troubleshooting@email.university.edu>
Subject: Re: Unable to View the Film Rashomon

Dear Dr. LeHane,
Thank you for your patience while we investigated this issue. We have worked with the video vendor and have had our library's access to *Rashomon* reinstated. The library lost access due to a misunderstanding regarding payment with the vendor—all of which has now been resolved. Please reach out in the future if you require assistance.

Kind regards,
Troubleshooter

ADDITIONAL READINGS AND RESOURCES

Emery, Jill, Graham Stone, and Peter McCracken. 2020. "Troubleshooting." In *Techniques for Electronic Resource Management: TERMS and the Transition to Open*, 91–116. Chicago: ALA Editions.

Hartnett, Eric, and Carole Thompson. 2010. "From Tedious to Timely: Screencasting to Troubleshoot Electronic Resource Issues." *Journal of Electronic Resources Librarianship* 22 (3–4): 102–12. doi:10.1080/1941126X.2010.535736.

Perkins, Jeffrey. 2008. "Solving Electronic Journal Problems Effectively: A Short Guide." *Journal of Electronic Resources in Medical Libraries* 5 (3): 267–73. doi:10.1080/15424060802222471.

Ross, Sheri V. T., and Sarah W. Sutton. 2016. "Providing Access to Electronic Resources." In *Guide to Electronic Resource Management*, 69–92. Santa Barbara, CA: Libraries Unlimited.

Verminski, Alana, and Kelly Marie Blanchat. 2017. "Keeping the Lights On: Setting Up and Maintaining Access." In *Fundamentals of Electronic Resources Management*, 99–130. Chicago: ALA Neal Schuman.

Zellers, Jessica, Tina M. Adams, and Katherine Hill. 2018. "I Think the Internet Broke." In *The ABCs of ERM: Demystifying Resource Management for Public and Academic Librarians*, 154–68. Santa Barbara, CA: Libraries Unlimited.

REFERENCE

Davis, Susan, Teresa Malinowski, Eve Davis, Dustin MacIver, Tina Currado, and
   Lisa Spagnolo. 2012. "Who Ya Gonna Call? Troubleshooting Strategies for
   E-resources Access Problems." *Serials Librarian* 62 (1–4): 24–32. doi:10.1080/03615
   26X.2012.652459.

6

Common Access Issues and Examples

Now that we have walked through the entire troubleshooting process, in this chapter we go through several examples from beginning to end. Their narratives are much shorter than those for the examples previously covered in chapters 3, 4, and 5. Table 6.1 presents the top ten common issues that are encountered with problem reports. This list is by no means comprehensive but can act as a reference tool by briefly summarizing solutions to common problems encountered by troubleshooters. Throughout this chapter, we include several different examples that correspond to these top ten common issues, as noted in table 6.1.

TABLE 6.1 Common issues and their solutions

Issue	Reason	Solution	Example
User error	The patron navigated to the resource from outside the library's access tools.	Educate the patron on how to access and use library e-resources.	
	The patron incorrectly interpreted a library's holdings.		
	The patron is unfamiliar with using features of library e-resources.		
	The patron is attempting to access a resource from the wrong browser or without the necessary software.		
	The patron is no longer an authorized user.		

(continued)

TABLE 6.1 Common issues and their solutions *(cont'd)*

Issue	Reason	Solution	Example
Vendor cut access	Your library does not have access to an e-resource due to a payment issue.	Work with the vendor and the library's acquisitions staff to process payment.	1
	The vendor incorrectly thought your library does not have access rights.	Contact the vendor to reestablish access on the platform.	
Incorrect e-resource implementation	Your library does not own or subscribe to the e-resource. You verify, via acquisitions or other records, that it should not have been made discoverable.	Remove the e-resource from discovery.	2
	Access was never established on the vendor platform when the e-resource was acquired.	Supply the vendor with the necessary information, such as IP addresses, to complete registration.	3
Broken or misdirecting link	Incorrect metadata in a link from the research guide, ILS, or database A–Z list leads to an error message or being directed to the wrong content.	Navigate to the vendor platform to attempt to find the desired content elsewhere on the platform. Inform the patron of the alternate route. Change local records to reflect updates.	4, 5
	Incorrect metadata in a link from knowledge base or central index leads to an error message or being directed to the wrong content.	Navigate to the vendor platform to attempt to find the desired content elsewhere on the platform. Inform the patron of the alternate route. Whether or not you find the content via an alternate route, contact the e-resource or access tool vendor to update its metadata.	6, 7

Issue	Reason	Solution	Example
Broken or misdirecting link	The e-resource URL is outdated due to a vendor website architecture change or content being removed.	Contact the vendor of either the access tool or e-resource to alert the vendor of the outdated link with incorrect metadata.	8
	The e-resource record is used only for internal purposes and the access mechanism is not actively updated.	Suppress or otherwise hide the e-resource record from patron view.	9
Incorrect holdings	Holdings do not accurately represent the library's access entitlements: • incorrect coverage dates • missing titles the library has subscribed to or purchased • including titles not subscribed to or purchased by the library	Use acquisitions records, vendor title lists, or licenses, etc., to update your library's holdings within your access tools.	10, 11
Authentication: EZproxy	An EZproxy prefix was not added to an e-resource's URL; patrons are therefore hitting a paywall.	Add the EZproxy prefix to the e-resource's URL.	12
	An EZproxy prefix was erroneously added to an e-resource's URL; patrons are receiving an EZproxy error.	Remove the EZproxy prefix from the e-resource's URL.	
	The e-resource's stanza is not included in the EZproxy configuration file.	Add the EZproxy stanza to the EZproxy configuration file.	
	The stanza for the e-resource in the configuration file is incorrect, e.g., missing host or domain name.	Correct the EZproxy stanza in the EZproxy configuration file.	13

(continued)

TABLE 6.1 **Common issues and their solutions** *(cont'd)*

Issue	Reason	Solution	Example
Authentication: VPN	Your institution's IT department has implemented split tunneling for your institution's VPN. The VPN is no longer routing e-resource traffic through the VPN.	Explain to patrons that the VPN no longer works as it used to and that they should not use it to access e-resources. In addition, work with your IT department and explain how the issue is confusing and an inconvenience to patrons and library staff. IT staff may or may not choose to change how traffic is routed.	
Authentication: SSO	Your institution's name is missing from the WAYF list on the e-resource's website.	Contact the e-resource vendor to resolve this issue.	
Authentication: username/ password	The patron has not created a necessary account with a particular e-resource and is attempting to log in with the patron's library credentials.	Educate the patron on how to create the necessary account and use it in the future to access the e-resource.	14
	A vendor has reset the username/password required for your library to access an e-resource without notifying your library.	Update the username/ password for your patrons.	
Unauthorized text and data mining	A vendor has deliberately denied your library access to an e-resource due to unauthorized text and data mining.	Contact the patron to explain the situation and alert the patron of future requirements for compliance. Contact the vendor to explain that you have notified the patron of the unauthorized use.	

Example 1: Vendor Cut Access

SCENARIO

A library staff member forwards a ticket to the troubleshooter about a faculty member who is unable to view a streaming video. From the ticket, the troubleshooter learns the following:

> *who:* faculty member
> *what:* a streaming video
> *when:* all week
> *where:* off campus
> *how:* navigation to the video from a record in the discovery interface

ACCESS CHAIN

library website > discovery interface > direct link > proxy server > video on vendor platform

SOLVING THE PATRON-FOCUSED PROBLEM

The troubleshooter first attempts to re-create the issue by navigating to the record in the discovery interface and attempting to access the video, which the troubleshooter is unable to view, receiving instead a prompt to purchase the video. The troubleshooter is unable to offer a suggestion for an alternative mode of access to the video and so e-mails the faculty member that the troubleshooter is looking into the issue and will follow up with the faculty member later.

DIAGNOSING

The troubleshooter first checks acquisitions records to try to determine why there is a record for the streaming video in the library's discovery interface. The troubleshooter is able to find a record of purchase from 2016 for $200. The troubleshooter next contacts the vendor to inquire why the library's access has been cut. The vendor replies that the 2016 purchase was for a three-year license and if the library would like to reestablish access, it will need to purchase the title again for another three years.

RESOLUTION

Working with acquisitions staff, the troubleshooter's library decides to repurchase the streaming video title. Acquisitions staff note the three-year license in their records and the troubleshooter notifies the faculty member that access has been restored.

Example 2: Incorrect E-resource Implementation

SCENARIO

A faculty member is unable to access a database. From the troubleshooting interview, the troubleshooter learns the following:

who: faculty member
what: a database
when: Thursday
where: on campus
how: unable to access a database via the database A–Z list

ACCESS CHAIN

library website > database A–Z list > IP address authentication > database platform

SOLVING THE PATRON-FOCUSED PROBLEM

The troubleshooter attempts to access the database from the database A–Z list, and although taken to the database's homepage, the troubleshooter is denied access to any content. The troubleshooter is unable to offer an alternative mode of access to the database and so e-mails the faculty member that the troubleshooter will keep the faculty member updated.

DIAGNOSING

The troubleshooter then proceeds to check acquisitions records for the database to see if payment is up-to-date. The troubleshooter is unable to find any acquisitions records for the database.

RESOLUTION

After contacting an acquisitions staff member, the troubleshooter is told that the database in question was on trial for the past month. Acquisitions staff had unfortunately not yet made any records for the trial, and they were waiting for collection development staff to get back to them about whether the library would indeed subscribe to the resource.

The troubleshooter then e-mails collection development staff to inquire if the library will subscribe to the database so that the troubleshooter can inform the faculty member of the library's decision. After three days, a collection development staff member responds that, no, the library will not subscribe. The troubleshooter then removes the link to the database trial from the library's database A–Z list, informs the faculty member of the library's decision, and connects the faculty member with the appropriate subject liaison to work together to find another research solution.

Example 3: Incorrect E-resource Implementation

SCENARIO

A library staff member is wondering why the library does not have access to some e-books that were purchased several months ago. From the troubleshooting interview, the troubleshooter learns the following:

> *who:* library staff member
> *what:* e-books that were purchased several months ago
> *when:* Thursday
> *where:* on campus
> *how:* no access via MARC record to some e-books that were purchased
> several months ago

ACCESS CHAIN

library website > online catalog > direct link > IP address authentication > e-book platform

SOLVING THE PATRON-FOCUSED PROBLEM

The troubleshooter double-checks the catalog for the e-books in question and is also unable to access the content. The troubleshooter e-mails the library staff member to indicate that the issue is being investigated.

DIAGNOSING

Because the e-books are a recent acquisition, the troubleshooter checks the acquisitions records to see if anything is amiss. The troubleshooter does not find anything; the invoice was paid promptly.

RESOLUTION

The troubleshooter e-mails the e-book vendor to determine what is going on. The vendor confirms having received payment for the e-books. Because the issue is not obvious, the vendor asks the troubleshooter to log in to the library's administrative account to see if the e-book titles have appeared on the library account's holding list. The troubleshooter checks the generated report and notifies the vendor that the e-book titles are included; however, the troubleshooter reiterates that the library does not currently have access to the e-books.

Upon further investigation, the vendor determines that the wrong IP ranges were assigned to the e-book purchase—another institution was granted access to the e-books. The vendor corrects the internal error and the troubleshooter's library gains access to the e-books. The troubleshooter e-mails the reporter to notify the staff member that the e-books are now accessible.

Example 4: Broken or Misdirecting Link

SCENARIO

A patron reports a broken hyperlink for a database included on a research guide. From the troubleshooting interview, the troubleshooter learns the following:

who: student
what: 404 error message received when clicking on a hyperlink to the data-base
when: past few days
where: off campus
how: while accessing the history research guide, created by the library's liaison, as recommended by the student's history professor

ACCESS CHAIN

history research guide > proxy server > database platform

SOLVING THE PATRON-FOCUSED PROBLEM

The troubleshooter first re-creates the issue by navigating to the history research guide and testing the hyperlink. The troubleshooter also receives a 404 "Page not found" error message. Next, the troubleshooter attempts to access the database via an alternative route—in this case, via the library's database A–Z list. The troubleshooter is successfully able to access the content, so, after verifying that the student's account is in good standing, the troubleshooter provides the student with the working link. The troubleshooter also informs the student to check the database A–Z list for the most up-to-date resource links if the student encounters similar issues in the future.

DIAGNOSING

Because the troubleshooter was able to access the database via an alternative route, this is not an acquisitions or vendor platform issue. The troubleshooter goes to the research guide in question to compare the hyperlink's URL to that being used for the same database in the library's database A–Z list. Immediately the troubleshooter notices that the URLs do not match. This is likely because the research guide's creator made the hyperlink on the fly.

RESOLUTION

The troubleshooter then notifies the research guide's creator of the issue—including the need for the creator to update the link on the research guide before more help tickets come in—and reiterates standard procedure of using only existing assets when adding e-resource links to a research guide.

Example 5: Broken or Misdirecting Link

SCENARIO

A library staff member reports a broken database link in the library's database A–Z list. From the troubleshooting interview, the troubleshooter learns the following:

who: library staff member
what: a database link is broken in the database A–Z list
when: Tuesday
where: on campus
how: found while accessing the library's database A–Z list

ACCESS CHAIN

library website > database A–Z list > IP address authentication > database platform

Because this issue was submitted by an internal reporter and not on behalf of a patron, there is no patron-focused problem.

DIAGNOSING

The troubleshooter first re-creates the issue by testing the link in the database A–Z list. The troubleshooter is also unable to access the database. The troubleshooter decides to verify whether the database is accessible via an alternative route. Because the database is authenticated via IP address, the troubleshooter navigates to it via a search engine. The database is accessible. The troubleshooter then right-clicks the database A–Z link to examine the URL. The troubleshooter sees that the URL being used is not a static URL and includes a session identifier (ID).

RESOLUTION

The troubleshooter responds to the library staff member who reported the issue to explain the cause of the problem and assure the staff member that the link will be corrected. The troubleshooter corrects the link to a static one (obtained via the search engine) in the database A–Z list and then e-mails the staff member who originally created the entry a gentle reminder that links containing session IDs often break and that static URLs or permalinks are needed when creating database A–Z list entries.

Example 6: Broken or Misdirecting Link

SCENARIO

An off-campus student is unable to view an article from the *Journal of Photography*. The student is instead taken to an article about painting. From the troubleshooting interview, the troubleshooter learns the following:

> *who:* student
> *what:* an article link is broken in the discovery service
> *when:* Wednesday morning
> *where:* off campus
> *how:* misdirected to an incorrect article after clicking on a link while conducting a search in the discovery service

ACCESS CHAIN

library website > discovery service > article record > proxy server > link resolver > article on vendor platform

SOLVING THE PATRON-FOCUSED PROBLEM

The troubleshooter confirms that the article link from the discovery service is broken by trying it firsthand. The link for the *Journal of Photography* article does indeed misdirect to a different article about painting. The troubleshooter then wants to meet the reporter's immediate need by providing the student with the article in question. The troubleshooter attempts to access the article via the e-journal A–Z list and is successful. The troubleshooter then e-mails the student the article (after verifying the student is an active patron), thanks the student for reporting the issue, and indicates that the broken link will be addressed. The troubleshooter also explains to the student how to use the e-journal A–Z list to drill down to desired journal articles in case the student encounters any more broken article-level links from the discovery service in the future.

DIAGNOSING

The link on the article record is an OpenURL link, not a direct link. This means that either the metadata being used to construct the link was erroneous or the parser used by the link resolver is not functioning correctly. Unfortunately, the troubleshooter is unable to view the OpenURL itself to see what metadata was being parsed. However, regardless of whether it is an article-level metadata issue or a problem with the parser, the discovery services vendor will need to be contacted to correct the issue.

RESOLUTION

The troubleshooter contacts the discovery services vendor through its support portal to notify the vendor to update the discovery service's central index and knowledge base with updated metadata for the *Journal of Photography* article. The discovery services vendor responds that the misdirecting link will be updated.

Example 7: Broken or Misdirecting Link

SCENARIO

An on-campus student is unable to access an article from an e-journal. From the troubleshooting interview, the troubleshooter learns the following:

> *who:* student
> *what:* an e-journal
> *when:* weekend
> *where:* on campus
> *how:* unable to access a 2017 article in an e-journal via the discovery service

ACCESS CHAIN

library website > discovery service > article record > link resolver > IP address authentication > article on vendor platform

SOLVING THE PATRON-FOCUSED PROBLEM

The troubleshooter attempts to access the article from 2017 and is unable to do so. The e-journal A–Z list shows that the library should have holdings from v.1(1930)–present. The troubleshooter notices that the e-journal's homepage features a message stating that the e-journal is migrating platforms, from one publisher to another, and also notices a link at the top to the new publisher's platform. The troubleshooter attempts to access the same e-journal content on the new publisher's platform and is able to access the 2017 article. The troubleshooter, after verifying that the student has an active account, e-mails the student the 2017 article. The troubleshooter explains that the e-journal's platform has recently changed and that the library's records will be updated soon.

DIAGNOSING

The troubleshooter next checks for all of the library's access on the new publisher's platform because the library's e-journal A–Z list currently indicates that the library should have access to v.1(1930)–present of the e-journal. The library does not have access to any years of content beyond the current subscription on the new publisher's platform. To cover all the bases, the troubleshooter then checks acquisitions records looking for proof that the library should have access to the back-file years, which represent the content from v.1(1930) to the beginning of the current subscription. The troubleshooter is able to find a record that the library bought the back-files of the e-journal in 2013 for $20,000.

RESOLUTION

The troubleshooter first contacts the library's LSP provider to notify the provider that the link for the e-journal in the knowledge base needs to be updated due to the publisher change. The LSP provider then informs the library that it will need to receive the metadata required for the update from the new publisher.

The troubleshooter then contacts the new publisher of the e-journal to (a) have the library's back-file access restored and (b) inform the publisher that it is necessary to provide updated metadata to the library's LSP provider for the knowledge base. In the end, after receiving proof of payment, the publisher restores the library's back-file access on the new publisher's platform, and the LSP provider updates the knowledge base with the correct link.

Example 8: Broken or Misdirecting Link

SCENARIO

An off-campus student is unable to view an article from the *Journal of Art*. From the troubleshooting interview, the troubleshooter learns the following:

> *who:* student
> *what:* an article link is broken in the discovery service
> *when:* Saturday night
> *where:* off campus
> *how:* broken article link from the *Journal of Art* discovered while conducting a search in the discovery service

ACCESS CHAIN

library website > discovery service > article record > proxy server > link resolver > article on vendor platform

SOLVING THE PATRON-FOCUSED PROBLEM

The troubleshooter first confirms that the article link from the discovery service is broken by trying it firsthand. The troubleshooter then wants to meet the reporter's immediate need by providing the student with the article in question. The troubleshooter attempts to access the article via the e-journal A–Z list but discovers that the title-level link is broken there as well. At this point, the troubleshooter attempts to navigate to the journal by using a search engine to pull up the *Journal of Art*'s homepage. The troubleshooter is able to do so and is recognized as a subscriber because the troubleshooter is on campus. The troubleshooter then downloads the article in question and e-mails it to the student (after verifying the student is an active patron). The troubleshooter also explains how to access the e-journal both on and off campus because the journal's links will be broken on the library's access tools until a resolution is reached. The student can access the journal on campus by searching for the *Journal of Art* with a search engine; because the search is being conducted on campus, the student will be recognized as an authorized user. In order to be recognized by the journal's publisher as an authorized user from off campus, the student will need to first connect via VPN and then navigate to the journal's platform via a search engine.

DIAGNOSING

To diagnose the issue, the troubleshooter compares the *Journal of Art*'s URL, navigated to previously via a search engine, to the URL being used by both the library's e-journal A–Z list and its discovery service. The troubleshooter notices that the URL on the e-journal's platform does not match what is being used by the library's e-journal A–Z list and discovery service. At this point, the publisher's name rings a bell in the troubleshooter's mind. Sure enough, the publisher had e-mailed the library's contact person the week before to notify the library that the publisher was implementing drastic website updates.

RESOLUTION

At this point, the troubleshooter needs to contact the library's LSP vendor, which controls the knowledge base that populates the e-journal A–Z list and the discovery service, to notify the vendor to update the LSP's knowledge base with the new link for the *Journal of Art*. The troubleshooter then contacts the LSP vendor to explain the issue. The LSP vendor responds that no updates have been received from the *Journal of Art*'s publisher and that the library will need to inform that publisher of the necessary updates to provide to the LSP vendor.

The troubleshooter then e-mails the *Journal of Art*'s publisher to explain the issue. In reply, the publisher informs the troubleshooter that the appropriate updates have already been sent to the LSP vendor. At this point, several days have passed since the original incident was reported, and the library is receiving multiple tickets per day about this particular publisher's platform. The troubleshooter thus informs the library's web team, the staff in charge of the library's website, to place a banner on the library's homepage that will inform patrons of the known issue.

The troubleshooter then relays what the *Journal of Art*'s publisher said back to the LSP vendor. The LSP vendor acquiesces, indicating that the updates will be pushed out in the next monthly release, in two weeks' time. The troubleshooter enacts the appropriate calendar reminder for follow-up. Weeks later, the troubleshooter follows up with the library's web team to remove the homepage banner after confirming that the issue has been resolved.

Example 9: Broken or Misdirecting Link

SCENARIO

An on-campus student has found a database link that is broken. From the troubleshooting interview, the troubleshooter learns the following:

who: student
what: a database link is broken in the library catalog
when: Monday morning
where: on campus
how: discovered while conducting a search in the library catalog

ACCESS CHAIN

library website > online catalog > direct link > IP address authentication > database platform

SOLVING THE PATRON-FOCUSED PROBLEM

The troubleshooter is able to confirm that the library catalog record does indeed have an outdated/broken database link. In an e-mail, the troubleshooter apologizes to the patron, indicating that the record the patron found should not have been available and had an outdated link. The troubleshooter also mentions that in the future the student should use the library's database A–Z list (link included in e-mail) to find available databases because the A–Z list will always have the most up-to-date links.

DIAGNOSING

Going back to the MARC record for the database within the ILS, the trouble-shooter notices that the record is very brief and assumes that it is likely used for acquisitions purposes. The troubleshooter also knows that the library no longer maintains individual records for databases within the library catalog but instead directs patrons to use the library's database A–Z list to discover databases.

RESOLUTION

The troubleshooter suppresses the record in question so that it is no longer discoverable by patrons.

Example 10: Incorrect Holdings

SCENARIO

A student is unable to access an article from the *Journal of Geology*. From the troubleshooting interview, the troubleshooter learns the following:

> *who:* student
> *what:* an article from the *Journal of Geology*
> *when:* Tuesday morning
> *where:* off campus
> *how:* unable to access a 2019 article from the *Journal of Geology* from the e-journal A–Z list

ACCESS CHAIN

library website > e-journal A–Z list > proxy server > e-journal platform > article on platform

SOLVING THE PATRON-FOCUSED PROBLEM

The troubleshooter attempts to access the article in question by navigating through the e-journal A–Z list. The troubleshooter is able to access the *Journal of Geology*'s homepage but unable to access the 2019 content. Because the student mentioned needing the article ASAP, the troubleshooter refers the student to interlibrary loan. In addition, the troubleshooter tells the student that the library's record will be updated accordingly once it is determined if the library actually subscribes to the *Journal of Geology*. The troubleshooter is also sure to inform interlibrary loan staff that they should push the request through even though it appears that the library has access to the 2019 article, according to the holdings listed in the library's e-journal A–Z list.

DIAGNOSING

The troubleshooter then attempts to check acquisitions records for the *Journal of Geology* and is unable to find any. The troubleshooter does find additional records for other e-journals to which the library subscribes through the *Journal of Geology*'s publisher. The troubleshooter then thinks to compare the library's tracked holdings with the title list found in the acquisitions records—maybe the *Journal of Geology* has been turned on by mistake.

RESOLUTION

Upon comparing the publisher's title list from the library's acquisitions records to what has been selected as holdings in the library's link resolver, the troubleshooter finds an additional two titles tracked that are not mentioned in the library's acquisitions records. The troubleshooter goes to one of these journals' homepages to determine if the library has access to the content. The troubleshooter finds that the library does have access to this second e-journal and sees in the publisher's title information on the e-journal's homepage the following information: "This e-journal will remain open access for its first two years of publication (2019 and 2020), after which a subscription will be required to access content from 2021 on."

The troubleshooter then wonders if the same parameters are true for the *Journal of Geology*. Checking the publisher's title information for the *Journal of Geology*, the troubleshooter finds a similar notice: "This e-journal will remain open access for its first two years of publication (2017 and 2018), after which a subscription will be required to access content from 2019 on."

At this point, the troubleshooter has determined that the library no longer has access to the *Journal of Geology* and so believes it wise to forward the relevant information to collection development staff so they can determine if a subscription to the journal should be started. If the library cared enough to track these temporary open access titles to begin with and the library subscribes to other journals from the same publisher, then perhaps the library would be interested in starting a subscription. The troubleshooter will then update the library's holdings accordingly, depending on the response from collection development.

Example 11: Incorrect Holdings

SCENARIO

A student is unable to access a 2017 entry in the e-book *The Food Encyclopedia*. From the troubleshooting interview, the troubleshooter learns the following:

who: student
what: a 2017 entry in the e-book *The Food Encyclopedia*
when: Friday afternoon
where: on campus
how: unable to access a 2017 entry in the e-book *The Food Encyclopedia* via a
    discovery service search result

ACCESS CHAIN

library website > discovery service > direct link > IP address authentication > e-book platform

SOLVING THE PATRON-FOCUSED PROBLEM

The troubleshooter attempts to access the same encyclopedia entry as did the student by conducting a discovery service search and then navigating using the e-book link. The troubleshooter is taken to the e-book's web page but is unable to access the 2017 entry. Because the student mentioned needing the encyclopedia entry ASAP, the troubleshooter refers the student to interlibrary loan. In addition, the troubleshooter tells the student that hopefully the discovery service search result will be updated in the future, depending on if it is determined that the library should have access. The troubleshooter is also sure to inform interlibrary loan staff that they should push the request through even though it appears that the library should have access to the e-book.

DIAGNOSING

The troubleshooter then wants to check acquisitions records to make sure that payment for the e-book is up-to-date. The troubleshooter finds that the library made a payment for the e-book in 2012 of $1,000. The troubleshooter returns to the e-book's platform and is able to access several encyclopedia entries but, at the same time, is denied access to other entries.

RESOLUTION

The troubleshooter is now at a loss to explain why the library does not have access to the reported 2017 entry as well as the other inaccessible entries the troubleshooter encountered. The troubleshooter now contacts the e-book's vendor to inquire what the library should have access to given the 2012 payment—which could represent either one year's subscription price or a one-time purchase amount. The vendor responds that the 2012 payment was a one-time purchase for only content produced up until that point and did not cover future updates to *The Food Encyclopedia*.

After coordinating with collection development staff, the troubleshooter's library decides to pay for the updates to *The Food Encyclopedia* since 2012, thereby enabling the content for patrons. The troubleshooter contacts the student to explain that the library's access to the desired content has now been established.

Example 12: Authentication—EZproxy

SCENARIO

A patron is unable to access an e-journal via the hyperlink on a library liaison's psychology research guide. From the troubleshooting interview, the troubleshooter learns the following:

who: student
what: student encounters a lock symbol and "Recommend for purchase"
    message on the vendor platform
when: Sunday afternoon
where: at the student's home off campus
how: encountered after clicking a hyperlink on a library liaison's psychology
    research guide

ACCESS CHAIN

psychology research guide > EZproxy server > e-journal on vendor platform

SOLVING THE PATRON-FOCUSED PROBLEM

The troubleshooter first re-creates the issue by navigating to the research guide and testing the hyperlink. The troubleshooter is able to access the e-journal and view its contents. Next, the troubleshooter verifies the student's account is in good standing before providing the student with instructions on how to access the e-journal via the e-journal A–Z list and recommending this route if the student encounters similar issues in the future.

DIAGNOSING

Because the troubleshooter was able to access the e-journal via the research guide's hyperlink from on campus, the issue is not the result of incorrect holdings or a problem with the vendor platform. The troubleshooter wants to check on the authentication for the link. The troubleshooter right-clicks the e-journal link on the research guide to view the full URL to make sure it has the necessary EZproxy prefix. It does not.

RESOLUTION

The troubleshooter notifies the research guide creator about the issue, taking the time to educate the creator on how to affix an EZproxy prefix to a link and to offer to answer any questions the person may have about the process.

Example 13: Authentication—EZproxy

SCENARIO

An on-campus library staff member has found a broken e-journal link within the library's e-journal A–Z list. From the troubleshooting interview, the troubleshooter learns the following:

who: library staff member
what: an EZproxy error message when accessing the *Journal of Philosophy* from the e-journal A–Z list
when: Thursday afternoon
where: on campus
how: stumbled upon a broken e-journal link in the library's e-journal A–Z list while doing personal reference work

ACCESS CHAIN

library website > e-journal A–Z list > EZproxy error message

Because the issue was submitted by an internal reporter and not on behalf of a patron, there is no patron-focused problem. The troubleshooter responds to the library staff member to thank that person for reporting the issue and to indicate that it will be followed up on. The library staff member mentioned not needing any further content, so the troubleshooter does not follow up with the reporter on an alternative way of accessing the *Journal of Philosophy* on campus.

DIAGNOSING

The library staff member included a screenshot of the error message received when trying to access the *Journal of Philosophy* on the John Smith Publishing platform. Based on the screenshot, the troubleshooter immediately knows that this is likely a proxy issue—the screenshot shows the library's standard EZproxy error page. The troubleshooter then goes into the configuration file for the library's EZproxy server and sees the following:

```
T John Smith Publisher
URL https://home.johnsmith.org
HJ ethics.johnsmith.org
HJ philosophy.johnsmith.org
HJ probability.johnsmith.org
DJ johnsmith.org
```

When comparing the stanza from the EZproxy configuration file to the current URL on the platform—https://johnsmith.org/philosophy—the troubleshooter thinks that perhaps the publisher is no longer using host names in its website architecture. The troubleshooter clicks around a little more on the publisher's platform to confirm this suspicion. The troubleshooter verifies that for the *Journal of Ethics* the link is now https://johnsmith.org/ethics.

RESOLUTION

The troubleshooter, upon confirming that the publisher is no longer using host names, updates the EZproxy stanza to the following:

```
T John Smith Publisher
URL https://home.johnsmith.org
DJ johnsmith.org
```

Example 14: Authentication—Username/Password

SCENARIO

An off-campus faculty member is unable to access a database prominent in the professor's field. From the troubleshooting interview, the troubleshooter learns the following:

who: faculty member
what: unable to log in to a database
when: Saturday
where: off campus
how: navigated to the database from a search engine and attempted to log in using institutional credentials

ACCESS CHAIN

search engine > database platform homepage

SOLVING THE PATRON-FOCUSED PROBLEM

The troubleshooter knows that the database in question requires authorized users to visit a special homepage to create a user account while within campus IP ranges. Once the user has established an account, the user can then access the database whenever/wherever, such as via a browser bookmark or search engine. The library has attempted to mitigate the issue by creating a special homepage for the database. Instead of being taken directly to the database from the library's database A–Z list, the patron is first taken to the special landing page that directs the patron either to click through to log in with a personal account or, if the patron does not have an account, to first establish a user account to receive access to the database. Despite the addition of the landing page, access issues with this database are commonly reported due to confusion about creating the necessary account.

DIAGNOSING

Because the faculty member mentioned using institutional credentials when attempting to log in to the database, the troubleshooter recognizes that this is an authentication issue. By providing the faculty member with the correct instructions to sign up for an account, the authentication issue should be resolved.

RESOLUTION

The troubleshooter e-mails the faculty member about the need to access the database from the library's database A–Z list in order to view the web page that provides detailed instructions about creating a user account. The troubleshooter provides a link to the database A–Z list and also explains that following creation of the required user account, the faculty member will be able to access the database from any chosen starting point.

7

Troubleshooting
Workflows and Training

Troubleshooting can be a very collaborative task. Although many libraries have several staff devoted to troubleshooting, some libraries have only enough resources to devote part of one staff member's time to troubleshooting. All library staff have a need for troubleshooting knowledge. Staff not directly involved in issue resolution still need to understand how to report issues. Throughout this chapter, we focus on collaborative troubleshooting with the hope that if you are the sole troubleshooter at your library, you will be inspired with new ideas on how to possibly involve others in order to ease the burden on yourself or how to collaborate on some aspect of your troubleshooting workflow. Although there are certainly varying, unlimited scenarios of staffing and the staff's base knowledge, throughout this chapter, we consider staff at three different levels of base knowledge—beginner, intermediate, and advanced—and discuss three main contributions to troubleshooting by these staff—reporting, diagnosing, and resolution. No matter how many people participate in the troubleshooting workflow at your library, even if the team and process do not fit the labels we have chosen to use for illustrative purposes, we hope that you can still glean insight that can be applied to your local workflow by identifying the necessary core competencies of your staff and possible areas of improvement for your workflow.

In the world of project management, the "12 Principles Behind the Agile Manifesto" by the Agile Alliance (2020) represent a popular approach for workflows that are under continuous pressure to never stop evolving. Originally designed for software development workflows, the manifesto and its principles address several concerns that are extremely applicable to the e-resource troubleshooting environment: "iterative planning and priority setting, regular workflow review for feedback, face to face communication, clearly defined project roles and deliverables, and keeping it simple" (Collins and Wilson 2018, 9). These concerns directly address the ever-changing nature of technology, troubleshooting methods, and troubleshooting staff turnover, issues that all libraries encounter:

> *Iterative planning and priority setting:* Troubleshooting workflows need to be regularly evaluated. A workflow designed one year ago may no longer be relevant due to technology or staffing changes.
>
> *Regular workflow review for feedback:* Troubleshooting workflows often do not behave as expected, and adjustments are necessary to cope with any changes. It is important to receive feedback from troubleshooting team members, other library staff, and patrons.
>
> *Face-to-face communication:* When training staff and designing the workflow, it is essential that body language and clarity of words be considered.
>
> *Clearly defined project roles and deliverables:* Troubleshooting workflows are most successful when staff, both within and outside of the immediate troubleshooting team, know their specific roles and responsibilities.
>
> *Keeping it simple:* This approach prevents troubleshooting workflows from ballooning with inefficiencies if attention to detail is ignored and if the workflow lacks focus.

Throughout this chapter, we highlight these concerns inspired by the agile project management model while addressing the basic tenets of project management: guiding principles, staff, accountability, workflow design, creating documentation and procedures, and training. The final section of the chapter addresses troubleshooting your troubleshooting workflow.

Guiding Principles

There are many routes and options when it comes to project management for an e-resources troubleshooting workflow. Just as your library or organization likely has its own mission statement setting out the underlying goals and priorities of the organization, you should consider creating guiding principles for your troubleshooting team. Guiding principles offer an opportunity to address the following concerns of agile project management: iterative planning and priority setting and clearly defined project roles and deliverables. Although this may seem silly or contrived at first, we have found that guiding principles help individuals act in alignment with their team's core values by fostering buy-in and a shared sense of agreement. Furthermore, in an interdepartmental environment, a troubleshooting team's guiding principles can be used to hold disparate team members accountable, bolster morale by reminding team members of the purpose of their daily work, and guide the team through tumultuous times of increasing change or indecision. Ultimately, a team's guiding principles should answer for team members the *why* in "Why do you do what you do?"

We are using the term *guiding principles* to encompass any directional documentation for a team, from a brief mission statement to a lengthy project charter. For established workflows, guiding principles can represent an ideal set of circumstances and reflect less on the workflow's current reality. Your guiding principles, in whatever form, are meant to reduce miscommunication, get everyone on the same page, guide troubleshooting team leaders in shepherding team members, provide accountability and transparency for team members, and specifically outline what your troubleshooting workflow intends to accomplish and what is outside of its scope. Be sure to develop your guiding principles as a group and revisit them both at regular meetings to reinforce their relevancy and annually to reassess if any team changes necessitate an update.

A project charter can be beneficial for new or established troubleshooting workflows, but it is particularly beneficial when a troubleshooting team needs assistance in advocating for resources from library leadership. Library leaders may be more amenable to devoting significant time or staffing resources to a troubleshooting workflow if they are able to see the team's overarching goals, impact on patrons, and potential risks from a bird's-eye view. A project charter is meant to be a comprehensive document. If you were ever to be contacted about your troubleshooting workflow by a librarian outside of your own library, you could potentially pass on your project charter to that person and thereby provide all the information that person would need to mimic your internal workflow. Project charters typically answer these questions:

- Who is a part of the troubleshooting team?
- What is the troubleshooting team setting out to do?
- Who will act as troubleshooting team leadership?
- What are the scope and impact of the troubleshooting workflow?
- Will there be any changes to existing workflows?
- Who will be impacted by any potential changes?
- With whom has the troubleshooting workflow been discussed?
- What are the desired outcomes of the troubleshooting workflow?
- What are the associated risks to achieving these desired outcomes?
- How will the success or impact of the workflow be measured?
- What are the specific steps and timeline for implementing the workflow?
- Are there any milestones regarding workflow implementation that can be measured?
- How does the troubleshooting workflow align itself with the library's strategic plan?

Project charters also create an inherent, detail-oriented team history, listing what resources—be they time, staff, or technology—have been required in the past to contribute to the success of the troubleshooting workflow. Especially in light of staff turnover, any future changes to an existing troubleshooting workflow can benefit from a detailed history of what decisions were made in the past and for what reasons. A project charter also fosters transparency and accountability among troubleshooting team members; this, in turn, promotes a high-level trust environment that directly contributes to the team's overall efficacy. Going beyond the immediate troubleshooting team purposes, a project charter can also be condensed and distributed to library-wide staff for transparent, informational purposes.

If you find yourself overwhelmed at the idea of creating a project charter given the current state of your existing or new troubleshooting workflow, a mission statement is an appropriate substitute that can accomplish many of the same goals as a project charter. Remember the agile project management concern of *keeping it simple*, and try to develop a useful mantra, in as few sentences as possible, that is relevant to your particular workflow on a day-to-day basis. Here is an example troubleshooting team mission statement:

> We exist to serve the library's patrons, to aid them in discovering library resources, and to assist them in any way within our power to make their library experience positive. While troubleshooting, we will make the best possible decision that we can with the information that we have in the moment. We will follow through on commitments and proactively reach out for assistance from fellow team members if we are struggling.

Staff

As mentioned in chapter 1, troubleshooting infrastructure and workflow play an important part in the effectiveness of access troubleshooting. The more staff a library is able to devote to the troubleshooting workflow, the more successful the library's customer service will be. We encourage you to think outside the box when identifying potential troubleshooting team members so you can devote as many staff as possible to your troubleshooting workflow.

When discussing staff in this chapter, we focus on the best practices for training three different groups of people to maintain a collaborative troubleshooting workflow: troubleshooting team members, frontline staff, and coworkers. These labels are meant to address both the various roles of staff and the various levels of troubleshooting knowledge necessary to participate in a troubleshooting workflow. The situation in your library may look different, with either a great amount of overlap in roles or inconsistencies in the knowledge of staff members within one group. For our illustrative purposes, it is most useful to break down the different needs and considerations of library staff into these three different groups:

> *Troubleshooting team members—advanced knowledge; capable of issue resolution:* This category represents staff who are able to fully submit, diagnose, and resolve problem reports. These staff members have access to all the information necessary for resolution, including acquisitions records, cataloging records, vendor contacts, and IT contacts. Team members can fix local issues as well as follow up with outstanding vendor issues, which are more likely to be drawn out over an extended time period.
>
> *Frontline staff—intermediary knowledge; capable of basic problem diagnosis:* This category represents any library staff—for example, circulation, reference, and access services staff—who are capable of diagnosing basic problem reports. These staff members likely encounter patrons frequently in their day-to-day work and are therefore the primary intermediaries between patrons and troubleshooting team members. This group is less likely to be a part of the troubleshooting team itself due to permissions issues, such as lacking access to acquisitions records, cataloging records, or a vendor contact list, that prevent these staff members from resolving most problem reports. Despite their lack of back-office access, frontline staff are often capable of some level of basic diagnosis.
>
> *Coworkers—beginning knowledge; capable of reporting:* This category represents any library staff—for example, library administration, archivists, and other internal reporters—who will not participate in diagnosing or resolving problem reports. Coworkers have a beginner's knowledge of troubleshooting and are responsible for understanding how to accurately submit problem reports. These staff members are less likely to encounter patrons frequently in their day-to-day work and do not often act as intermediaries between patrons and troubleshooting team members.

Although overlap of reporting, diagnosing, or resolution skills will certainly be prevalent, overall, attempt to identify who among your library staff falls into which category. A careful balance must be achieved on the troubleshooting team to account for rudimentary tasks, technical knowledge, leadership, accountability, and project management. Where possible, any troubleshooting team duties should be balanced with the staff's existing workload. Support staff, student assistants, or less experienced staff should likely be relied on to address issues at an entry level and should be trained to know when to escalate a ticket to more experienced staff. Professional or highly tech-savvy staff should likely focus more on complex issues, team management, and training, which are more effective uses of their time in the long run as compared to having them respond to easily resolved tickets in the trenches.

Troubleshooting Team Leads and Accountability

We recommend officially designating an individual as the troubleshooting team lead, or a group of individuals as troubleshooting team leads, to oversee the troubleshooting workflow of your library. With established guiding principles, troubleshooting team leads can actively hold team members accountable to their common goals while creating a shared vision of where the team is headed and what it will set out to achieve. Healthy troubleshooting team leads should incorporate in their daily work the following concerns of agile project management: face-to-face communication, clearly defined project roles, and *keeping it simple*. Team leads are responsible for maintaining the workflow, managing team dynamics, initiating training and/or continuing education, and completing assessment. They will envision your troubleshooting workflow from beginning to end, planning for any foreseeable roadblocks and prioritizing day-to-day tasks. They also proactively define goals, outcomes, assessment initiatives, and success metrics for your library's troubleshooting workflow. Ultimate responsibility for both small and large tasks falls on them; they can also delegate certain responsibilities as they see fit.

Given the common interdepartmental composition of troubleshooting teams, team leads can be selected from any available staff. Depending on your library's organizational structure and interdepartmental hierarchies, you may want to consider whether multiple team leads are necessary. A lack of accountability is common within troubleshooting workflows because staff often come from various library departments and are supervised by different department heads and various line managers. In these situations, it is crucial to decide ahead of time who will shoulder the mantle of responsibility as a team lead. Yes, teams can survive without designated leadership, but success can often be attributed to someone who cares about the overall workflow and who has the time and base knowledge of the entire operation to address any issues that will inevitably occur. For example, a successful troubleshooting workflow will not only respond to urgent fires as they pop up but also address backlog or back-burner projects that, when prioritized, contribute to the overall health of the troubleshooting team. Examples of backlog or back-burner projects include checking access reports, assessing team continuing education needs, and developing stronger training materials.

Becoming a good team lead or trainer is a lifelong process—there are highs and lows, and lots of experimentation and data gathering are required to improve leadership performance. Regularly scheduled personal reflection is recommended to keep track of the minutiae of leadership responsibilities and to prioritize team goals. Self-reflection can be aided by various tracking systems and requisite notes, for example:

- bullet journal: extremely customizable record for all tracking needs
- team calendar: best approach for scheduling necessary, cyclical tasks
- online to-do list: a running to-do list easily accessible from anywhere

Our number one recommendation to a troubleshooting team lead is to always check your own contribution before that of your team member when an issue arises. For example, it may be tempting to zero in on a team member's lack of performance if an issue arises. However, the appropriate response would be to first check your own contribution to the issue as a team lead: Has the team member been resourced properly? Have you been clear, concise, and compassionate with the staff member whose performance is lacking? Personal accountability is the dividing line between subpar team leads who survive the daily deluge and successful team leads who thrive despite difficulties because they know they have done their share of the necessary work.

When it comes to maintaining the workflow, team leads are responsible for creating and fostering documentation, communication, training, and assessment. Knowledge dissemination in all forms must be a high priority. Although we discuss these topics further later in this chapter, we want to reiterate here that team leads should not only create these very important facets of the troubleshooting workflow but also ensure the continued development of each facet. For example, initial training for new team members cannot often be avoided; however, continuing education for existing team members can easily be neglected due to competing priorities. Another example would be the incredible amount of follow-through necessary for proper assessment. Thorough assessment often yields conclusions that were not originally expected. It is not enough to assess current services and deliverables for *A* or *B*. Assessment often involves dealing with the *C* that is unexpectedly found, and team leads are in the perfect position to keep track of findings and adjust future goals as necessary. In the end, the ultimate goal of workflow maintenance is that everyone involved, including troubleshooting team members, frontline staff, and coworkers, knows the entirety of the workflow. All staff members have been given the resources they need to do their parts, the means to communicate with one another, and the avenues to ask for additional resources or assistance if necessary.

Although the responsibility of many troubleshooting team leadership tasks can be delegated on the fly, staffing issues in particular are best handled by a sole individual, preferably by someone who is already in an established leadership role within your library. The handling of issues on an ad hoc basis by whoever is available cannot always be avoided, but implementing and following through with the necessary accountability is best done by the same consistent person(s) so that staff members know what to expect before issues arise. Team members are also watching each other, and even when they themselves are compliant, their witnessing of how issues are handled affects their respect for team leadership and commitment to the team's overall workflow.

Many weak points in troubleshooting workflows can be attributed to staffing issues in regard to punctuality, innate ability, adaptability, motivation, and other sensitive soft skills with which a given staff member may struggle. Your team leads will be directly responsible for holding team members accountable to the expectations of your library's predefined workflow. They are to proactively identify and address problem areas within your troubleshooting life cycle. For example, if a team lead determines that an individual staff member is causing a disruption in the workflow, the team lead could then work with this individual to address the staff member's weaknesses in innovative ways so that the team may function better overall. If after follow-up, accountability, and additional training, an individual is unable to effectively address identified weaknesses within a reasonable time frame, the team lead is then responsible for deciding when to stop investing in this particular staff member and start looking for a replacement for the vacancy on the team.

Team leads can also be responsible for getting buy-in from library or organizational leadership and for maintaining the morale of troubleshooting team members. Morale is extremely important to cultivate; it eases the stress of everyday issues and can unite team members in their efforts and passion for contributing to the collective goal. Especially within a troubleshooting workflow, good morale can define the level of customer service that patrons receive. Do troubleshooting team members have low morale and are interested in completing only the bare minimum of tasks that a problem report initiates? Or are they enthused and committed enough to go above and beyond, when called for, to identify larger, systemic issues arising from the daily deluge of problem reports? Some ideas for how team leads can increase or positively develop team morale include the following:

> *Plan for time together not working:* Celebrate team birthdays as a group, and schedule other unstructured time for team members to socialize (e.g., around existing holidays or as quarterly opportunities).
>
> *Initiate a kudos system:* The configuration of the system can vary, but the purpose is to provide an opportunity for all team members to be able to recognize one another when they catch fellow team members doing a great job.
>
> *Encourage open communication at team meetings:* Team members should feel comfortable bringing issues they have encountered to the group for discussion.
>
> *Commit to transparency:* Open the floor at team meetings for frank discussions to address rumors and the like.
>
> *Practice follow-through:* When resourcing staff members, the more you can follow through and stay true to your word, the quicker trust will develop between you and your team members.

Allow for imperfection: Reinforce with team members that in a troubleshooting environment, it is okay to make mistakes, to think on their feet, and to do the best they can with the information they have in the moment.

Exercise initiative: Commit to continued training so staff can increase their confidence in their daily troubleshooting work. It is okay for team members to make mistakes only if they can then learn from you how to course correct in the future.

Boosting team morale directly correlates with an increase in the technical and customer service excellence that a troubleshooting team is able to offer to patrons.

Designing a Troubleshooting Workflow

In our experience, the best library troubleshooting workflows encompass all of the problem-solving concepts we have covered thus far; that is, they address the patron-focused problem and the technology-focused problem and effectively steer troubleshooters through the stages of problem solving. Unfortunately, very few workflows are actually formed in this manner. We have found that workflows often spring up around the culture, specific knowledge sets, or personalities in the library. In these instances, the workflow can become imbalanced and inconsistent, focusing too heavily on one particular aspect or predilection rather than on the process as a whole. This can lead to a great amount of frustration and difficulties, not just for the troubleshooting team members, but for patrons as well.

For example, a library may have a strong culture of customer satisfaction, concerned primarily with fulfilling the immediate needs of patrons. However, because the frontline staff members prioritize resolving only the patron-focused problem—that is, ensuring that patrons receive what they need—they may see no benefit in reporting small or unreproducible issues to their technical services department. In reality, there is actually a great benefit from reporting these small problems because they may indicate that a systemic technology issue is occurring and the larger issue can then be more rapidly diagnosed and resolved. Similarly, if the library culture is primarily concerned with fixing systemic technological issues rather than helping individual patrons, library staff members may consider an access issue resolved once reported, regardless of whether the patrons have actually achieved their goals. In either case, an unmet need still exists.

When evaluating your library's troubleshooting workflow, try to identify what, if any, imbalances exist. We recommend looking at the workflow from end to end and asking whether both the patron-focused problem and the technology-focused problem are being addressed, and if not, why. Questioning your existing decisions and assumptions will reap great benefits, helping you either to reinforce positive practices or to identify trouble areas that you previously were not resourced to improve. Try some basic brainstorming methods such as having current troubleshooting staff write down the following: their current trouble-shooting duties, what the troubleshooters believe to be your current workflow, what systems and data sources they frequently reference and for what reason, and any suggestions they may have for improving your current workflow.

If your organization does not currently have a troubleshooting workflow in place, the architects of your new workflow should discuss the reasons why a work-flow has not been previously implemented. Pain points or roadblocks need to be identified, addressed, and accounted for in the plans for your new troubleshoot-ing workflow. Common pain points often revolve around limited resources, orga-nization, direction, and accountability. A pain point assessment is also beneficial for existing troubleshooting workflows that need improvement. We go into more detail about how to begin to improve existing workflows in the Troubleshooting Your Troubleshooting Workflow section at the end of this chapter.

Concerning agile project management, workflow development directly addresses iterative planning and priority setting as well as *keeping it simple*. Embracing simplicity can be very effective for streamlining a troubleshooting workflow that could otherwise balloon with inefficiencies or focus on the wrong objectives. Workflow development, maintained by iterative planning and priority setting, can help mitigate any naturally occurring issues of focusing too much on either patron-focused or technology-focused problems as well as address the previously mentioned common workflow pain points. Creating a troubleshooting workflow with clearly defined project roles and deliverables can also help trouble-shooting team leads advocate with library leadership for additional resources for the troubleshooting workflow, gather buy-in from troubleshooting team mem-bers and other library staff, and have a road map of current and future processes that decreases burnout and cognitive load for everyone involved.

SYSTEMS FOR MANAGING PROBLEM REPORTS

A multitude of options are available to your library for gathering, organizing, and responding to patron problem reports. Commercial products, open source prod-ucts, existing ticketing systems from elsewhere in your organization, or even simply e-mail can be deployed in various ways to meet your unique, local needs. No matter which system is chosen, the following should be taken into account:

- Is this system financially feasible for the foreseeable future?
- How customizable is this system? Does it meet all of your basic require-ments for functionality?
- Is this system future-proof? Will it still serve your library well if needs evolve down the road?
- What data is automatically captured by this system and what data is self-reported?

- Does this system support your patrons' needs? That is, does it allow you to successfully commit to your guiding principles?
- If problem reports are received from outside of the system, such as via a phone call or an e-mail, can this information be easily entered into the system?

Beneficial workflows can be built around even the simplest of problem report systems. For example, a centralized troubleshooting team e-mail, such as erteam@institution.edu, can be more than sufficient for soliciting problem reports from patrons. A centralized e-mail represents a team list, similar to an electronic discussion list, whereby all members receive the same e-mails at the same time. In addition, a separate e-mail inbox can be configured in all team members' primary e-mail accounts to support searching the e-mail archive of the team e-mail.

With the goal of *keeping it simple* in mind, be sure to consider whether your current problem report system is meeting all of your troubleshooting team's needs. It is very common for libraries to employ a rudimentary ticketing system that tracks the bare minimum of information for a problem report and does not allow for the recording of ancillary data, which is often necessary to follow up on and resolve a problem report. In this common situation, it may be beneficial to add an additional tracking system into the workflow to help manage the ancillary data of your problem reports. An additional system could be a project management application such as Slack, Asana, or Microsoft To Do; these applications are ideal because they often facilitate a form of messaging or commenting that can be viewed by multiple troubleshooting team members. When adding an additional system to work in conjunction with an existing system, consider the following questions:

- How will we code/notate a problem report (e.g., "John Brown 12/2/19") in the additional system to facilitate retrieval in both systems?
- What information will we transfer to the additional system? Remember to *keep it simple*: use as little information as possible to differentiate one problem report form another to aid in easy retrieval from one system to the next.
- Will the additional system allow all troubleshooting members to view the details of all problem reports? This is extremely beneficial in the event of staff absences or turnover.
- Will the new workflow with the additional system be easy for troubleshooting team members to learn? Documentation is a must when populating more than one system with problem report information.

DEVELOPING A TROUBLESHOOTING WORKFLOW FLOWCHART

As previously mentioned, the ultimate goal of a troubleshooting workflow is for everyone involved to know the entirety of the workflow. Everyone has the resources they need to act alone and collaboratively and can access additional resources or assistance if necessary. One of the best ways to capture this information for widespread dissemination is via a flowchart. Flowcharts can accurately reflect the cause-and-effect nature of the various tasks that are generated when troubleshooting an issue from a single problem report. Figure 7.1 reflects a simple troubleshooting workflow in which problem reports are solicited solely via e-mail, while figure 7.2 reflects a complex troubleshooting workflow in which problem reports are received via e-mail, chat, and online form.

In the Additional Readings and Resources section at the end of this chapter, we also include several articles with case studies of libraries that are either implementing or updating their troubleshooting workflows. We recommend paying particular attention to libraries with similar staffing structures, e-resources, or access tools as your library.

DOCUMENTING A TROUBLESHOOTING WORKFLOW

Upon reflecting on your troubleshooting workflow and considering your own workflow flowchart(s), begin to document all decisions so that both the troubleshooting team and other library coworkers can benefit from the clarity and transparency that clearly defined project roles and deliverables provide. As with agile project management, any documentation created should be regularly reviewed for feedback. Troubleshooting team documentation should cover the following topics: the minute details of the workflow, team communications, what information will be disseminated outside of the team, and training or continuing education (which we discuss further in the next section). Here are some examples of troubleshooting workflow items that you may wish to document:

- troubleshooting team or other relevant meeting minutes
- training or continuing education documents
- troubleshooting team workflow
- troubleshooting team or other relevant staffing rosters
- staff roster for relevant data access permissions (acquisitions, cataloging, IT, etc.)
- FAQ page(s) for troubleshooting team members, frontline staff, coworkers, or patrons

The possibilities for managing these workflow items are limitless. Examples include e-mail, local shared drive, cloud storage, team web page (wiki, etc.), project management app (Evernote, Slack, Asana, Trello, etc.), and so on. Revisit the questions we recommend for evaluating a problem report system to assess which

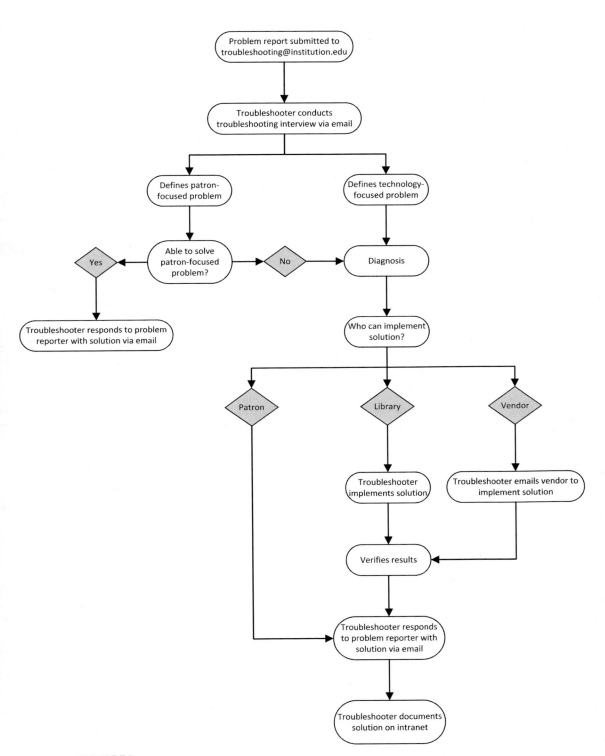

FIGURE 7.1
Simple troubleshooting workflow

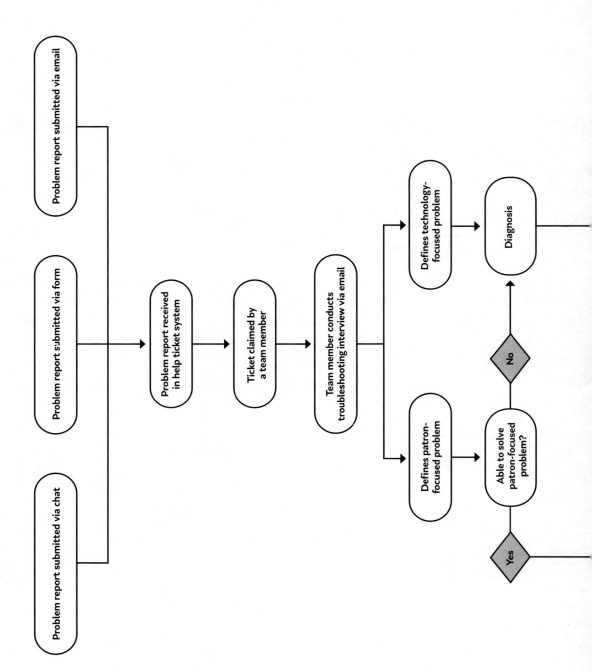

FIGURE 7.2
Complex troubleshooting workflow

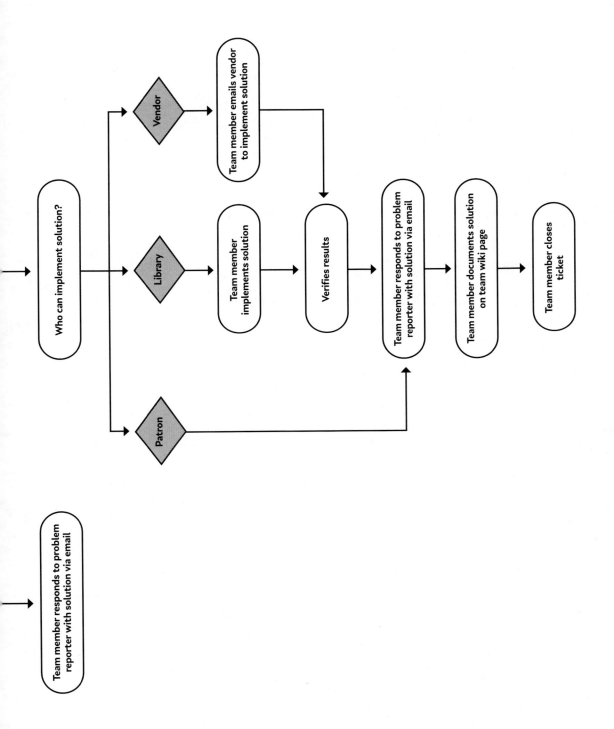

Who can implement solution?

Vendor

Team member emails vendor to implement solution

Library

Team member implements solution

Verifies results

Patron

Team member responds to problem reporter with solution via email

Team member documents solution on team wiki page

Team member closes ticket

Team member responds to problem reporter with solution via email documentation method could potentially best meet your troubleshooting team's current and future needs.

As an alternative to documenting the intricate details of a troubleshooting workflow via flowchart, team leads could map out a step-by-step process in a numbered list or checklist that a team member could then follow in a sequential fashion. A series of web pages on different topics could also serve as a useful day-to-day guide for certain troubleshooting topics, including team communication. Team communication can cover anything from monthly team meeting minutes to a weekly summary e-mail from team leads with good-to-know information. Documenting such communications can take several forms. For some purposes, such as casual, weekly e-mail updates, this information does not need to be stored outside of the recipients' e-mail inboxes. When more formal and long-lasting communications are created, however, this information should likely be stored in a centralized location where team members can easily access the documentation. Example centralized locations include an organization's shared drive, a team web page, or other productivity apps. Any part of the workflow that cannot be easily documented needs to be regularly reiterated by leadership in casual one-on-ones and at standing group meetings.

Beyond the direct documentation needs of the troubleshooting team discussed thus far, you should also consider what documentation, if any, needs to be disseminated library-wide and to patrons. Library coworkers sometimes find context for the library's troubleshooting workflow helpful and educational; sharing your troubleshooting workflow with others allows them to understand the great amount of work required to maintain e-resources and may encourage them to take their duty of reporting more seriously. Also, some libraries find it helpful to create brief web pages for patrons that feature answers to frequently asked questions. This information can often be found on the same web page with the library's online problem report form. Helpful information could include how to reset a password with campus IT, how to log on to the VPN, contact information for various library departments, or how to clear a browser's cache and cookies.

> ### Troubleshooting Tip: Advertising Troubleshooting Services to Patrons, Frontline Staff, and Coworkers
>
> For everyone's benefit, ensure that all avenues of advertising your trouble-shooting team's services been taken advantage of, including the library's website, the library's access tools, organizational websites, and word of mouth from library staff. For the benefit of library staff, consider any department standing meetings that could benefit from having an opportunity to ask troubleshooting questions with a troubleshooting team member. For example, an annual training day is a regular opportunity at which the troubleshooting team members can advertise their services to their coworkers.

Training for Troubleshooters

TRAINING TROUBLESHOOTING TEAM MEMBERS

No matter your library's troubleshooting team configuration, training documentation is always the best first step to improving your processes. With documentation in place, you can save a great amount of time during initial staff training and you are prepared in the event of staff turnover. Less communication is necessary to maintain daily workflows when you establish a culture that values documentation. Team leads can use robust documentation to transfer their domain knowledge, and troubleshooting team members can help themselves gain independence, knowing that they can depend on documentation to assist them when necessary. Creating successful documentation requires back-and-forth between both team leads and team members as they initiate adding to existing documentation or creating completely new documentation. For the team leads who are doing the training, it is especially important to receive regular feedback on the training documentation from team members. Oftentimes, team trainers have such an established base knowledge of troubleshooting that they find it difficult to put themselves in a new team member's shoes and remember what it was like learning to cope with complicated processes and rapidly changing technology.

We covered most of the base knowledge required for successful troubleshooting in our previous chapters, but Sunshine Carter and Stacie Traill (2017) provide an excellent summary of essential knowledge needed to successfully troubleshoot access problems:

- Overview of discovery and access environment
- Common points of failure
- Authentication and authorization
- OpenURL and link resolvers
- Differences and similarities between access for OA [open access]/free resources and licensed/paid resources
- Discovery index content, activations, and linking mechanisms
- Metadata sources, quality, and impact on access
- Detailed interaction between link resolver, discovery index, discovery layer, and LMS
- Distinguishing isolated issues from widespread problems
- Effective communication with system vendors and content providers (6)

When training troubleshooting team members on these concepts, we recommend using draft documentation and then updating the documentation with team member feedback. Repeat this process with several different trainees and keep adding to the document. Your training document may grow to be very long and literal; however, this level of detail will help create autonomy for team members by reducing the number of questions they have while completing a task. Team members can view the same task in different ways, and by incorporating their recommendations into team documentation, any future team members who approach the work from the same point of view will be addressed. Especially for those team members who are hesitant to stand on their own feet and who struggle with self-confidence or building their own troubleshooting base knowledge, very literal documentation can help to calm their sense of being overwhelmed because they will then know what to do at any given moment.

As mentioned earlier, any team training that cannot be easily documented should be regularly reiterated by trainers in casual settings and at more formal meetings. Face-to-face communication is very important when training troubleshooting team members. Various documentation formats could meet your training needs:

> *Physical binders for troubleshooting team members:* These are good for storing printouts of certain documents so that team members can add their own notes, with the caveat that they need to keep track of any updates that are made to the electronic versions of the documents. Example uses:
> > » basic training information on your library's access chain and authentication method(s)
> > » contact information and defined roles for coworkers with whom employees will need to collaborate
> > » information to include in vendor support portal tickets
>
> *Local shared drive, cloud storage, or a team web page (wiki, etc.):* Electronic documentation should be stored in a central repository that team members can access from any computer. Example uses:
> > » previously mentioned physical documentation examples
> > » collection of links to relevant training materials from your access tool vendors
> > » step-by-step instructions or checklists for common troubleshooting tasks
> > » e-resource vendor administration usernames and passwords
> > » instructions on how to navigate to acquisitions information via your access tools

Screencast videos with voice-over instructions from a trainer: These videos can be time-consuming to produce, but the amount of future time that they can potentially save is immeasurable. Example topics:

  » how to navigate access tools
  » how to make changes to settings in various websites, such as a vendor administrative site
  » how to diagnose issues by clicking around to various points in your library's access chain

In the Additional Readings and Resources section at the end of this chapter, we include several libraries' troubleshooting research guides for you to use to jump-start your imagination for what would work best for your troubleshooting workflow. Keep in mind that many of these examples are for the benefit of library patrons. However, a similarly formatted research guide could easily be created exclusively for your troubleshooting team.

Whether or not your troubleshooting team leads also serve as the trainers for your team, the previous recommendations we made for team leadership involving personal accountability and self-reflection are also applicable to troubleshooting team trainers. You might also consider shadowing between trainers and trainees as a part of your onboarding process. We also highly recommend peer-peer shadowing on your troubleshooting team. Where appropriate, ensure that you have proactively discussed this arrangement with any team member who will be training a peer. You should address the following:

  • whether the team member feels comfortable training a peer
  • that the team member is not expected to replace or have the same responsibilities as existing team trainers
  • that the peer trainer can stop the training if the peer trainee becomes unreasonable for any reason, with the responsibility returning to the existing team trainers

When training your troubleshooting team, be sure to account for different learning styles, personalities, and predilections. It is best to have the same expectations of all team members, but this can sometimes be tricky, especially if you have unique staffing issues, such as the following:

  • a team member who does not like to speak on the phone to patrons
  • a team member who is particularly flummoxed when updating EZproxy and therefore avoids this task
  • a team member who has a predilection for focusing on correcting electronic holdings and neglects other more pressing tasks as a result

It is your job as a trainer to identify and then address these weaknesses in team members through extra one-on-one training time, which can include the team member shadowing the trainer. Sometimes exceptions can be made, such as one team member not answering phone calls, without it negatively impacting the overall team's performance. However, because e-resource troubleshooting itself requires an aptitude for being open to learning new technology, ideas, and methods, trainers should still attempt to address these unique staffing issues. The ultimate goal is to foster an environment where all team members respond positively to change—which is easier said than done.

Trainers should also keep track of what team members know through either physical notes or online tracking—very similar to the notes team leads should keep about team goals and personal leadership. Some items to keep track of include topics covered, areas needing improvement, and peer-peer training needs. These are extremely brief notes (e.g., "John—proxy" and "Jane—e-mailing vendor for title list") and should be reviewed regularly—for example, given a brief glance over your morning coffee. Regularly reviewing your notes will jog your memory as a trainer when a relevant problem report occurs that you need to review either as a group or with a particular individual who has struggled in the past to understand the pertinent issue represented by the problem report. You may also want to add to these notes when you see a teaching opportunity in the form of a particular problem report: if you know that your team is struggling overall with a particular concept, you can claim the problem report yourself and document the steps you take in diagnosing and resolution as a teaching aid for the group.

Trainers can positively impact a troubleshooting team's morale by reminding the team members of the far-reaching ripple effects created by their daily work. Some people can find troubleshooting tedious and the minutiae of details to keep track of overwhelming. Troubleshooting work is also extremely frustrating and represents one of the few areas in life where knowledge mastery, even for team leads or trainers, is unlikely to occur within the foreseeable future. Given all these reasons, it can be very helpful for your troubleshooting team's morale to remind team members of the impact that their daily work has not only on the library's immediate patrons but possibly on a global scale as well. Especially if team members are completely new to e-resource work, they may pick up how to edit knowledge bases or contact vendors quickly, but they may not immediately grasp the larger importance that these small, but necessary, tasks represent. As a trainer, remind your trainees, where applicable, that the issues they are working on with vendors to correct affect all of that vendor's clients or subscribers. Remind them, too, of how much money is being spent on your library's e-resources, how many of your patrons are remotely based and therefore forced to use only e-resources, and be sure to share any thank-you notes or other patron outreaches of gratitude with the team as a whole.

Successful training includes teaching troubleshooters how to follow through and follow up on individual tasks that mushroom from a single problem report. One of the most crucial aspects of troubleshooting is seeing these generated tasks through to completion. For example, a single problem report may require (a) looking up local acquisitions information; (b) reaching out to a local contact, such as campus IT; (c) relaying information from campus IT to the e-resource vendor; (d) completing the steps recommended by the vendor to address an issue; and (e) following up with the patron after the issue has been addressed. In this example, several weeks could have passed from step *a* to step *e*, with several days passing in between each step. Similar to the brief notes we encourage trainers to use to keep track of the topics covered with staff, for example, this same form of brief note taking can be employed to track follow-up for problem reports. Here is the task sequence for the example just mentioned:

11/1 checked acqu data, we are up to date on payment. Contacted IT help desk

11/4 IT resp that they upd proxy, e-res still not available, 11/4 contacted vendor

11/9 vendor resp with upd proxy info, contacted IT to upd

11/10 e-res now available, notified patron

This type of note taking is especially helpful when keeping track of tasks that have been delegated to third parties; with multiple ongoing problem reports, it is extremely useful to see, at a glance, if you ever received a response from the inquiry you sent several days earlier. This information could be tracked in a help ticket system, a bullet journal, or an online to-do list or in an ancillary system, such as the project management apps we mentioned previously. Ideally, the information would be available to all troubleshooting team members to ensure follow-up in the case of staff absences, but this is not always possible in all systems. In addition, depending on the size of your troubleshooting team and the volume of problem reports your library receives, brief notes regarding who has done what and when might not be as crucial as they are in larger troubleshooting team environments.

When troubleshooters do not know what next step to take, stopping to consider what small task can be attended to in the meantime is very important. They need to remember to do as much as possible while waiting to receive additional instructions, when they are next able to connect with either peers or trainers. Keeping this in mind can often relieve much of the anxiety troubleshooters may experience about not knowing how to handle a particular problem report. Given the difficult nature of troubleshooting, troubleshooters often need to have *success* explicitly defined for them by their trainers. Examples of success could include the following:

- responding to a patron problem report that the issue will be looked into and then following up with a trainer about what to do next as soon as possible
- checking every possible issue that could be to blame for a problem report and still coming up short for an answer
- contacting a vendor and determining later on that this was unnecessary

Many of these successes may seem misguided to the uninitiated; however, a good trainer will express to team members how the results of certain actions are less important than the effort behind those actions. Team members should ultimately feel confident and know that they succeed when they make the best possible decisions that they can with the information they have in the moment.

TRAINING FRONTLINE STAFF

Frontline staff have intermediary knowledge and are capable of basic problem diagnosis. They also need to receive the same training on reporting as coworkers do, which we cover in the next section. Although frontline staff are capable of basic problem diagnosis, this does not guarantee that all frontline staff will either feel comfortable diagnosing or have the morale necessary to proactively engage with an encountered access issue. Uncomfortable frontline staff are more likely to pass on a problem report without giving any further thought to whether they could attempt to diagnose the access issue. Given that frontline staff regularly interact directly with patrons, it can be extremely helpful for a library's troubleshooting workflow if they are encouraged and resourced to develop their base troubleshooting knowledge that then aids their basic diagnostic skills. For example, whereas a coworker might stop at a broken article-level link in a discovery service because that person may not know how to access the article via an alternative route, a frontline staff member may learn through repeated experiences that the next best approach to accessing an article is via the library's e-journal A–Z list. Tips and tricks like this example save both frontline staff and patrons some frustration. Here are some additional examples:

- recommending that patrons try to clear their browser caches and cookies, then switch browsers, when first addressing an issue
- knowing what e-book platforms generate the most questions from patrons
- knowing what e-resources require the creation of an account or the use of a specific browser
- recognizing an EZproxy error when described by a patron

All of these scenarios provide an example of a time when the patron's need can quickly be met by a frontline staff member, if that staff member has the right base knowledge. You may find it useful to create for frontline staff an online FAQ with this type of information.

When collaborating with frontline staff, team leads should account for staff turnover and schedule regular continuing education opportunities for existing staff. Remember that there are likely many staff who work physical service desks outside of normal business hours. Think creatively about how you can deliver the same training, continuing education, and opportunities to connect with the troubleshooting team for further questions to these staff that you do for staff who work normal business hours.

TRAINING COWORKERS

Coworkers have beginning knowledge and are capable of reporting. Training for staff in your library whose roles are similar to our definition of coworker should focus solely on building their reporting skills. As Katherine A. Hart and Tammy S. Sugarman (2016) state:

> In the end, the public services employees did not have to learn to resolve tickets themselves, but rather understand the system and grasp the complexity of access issues to provide better diagnostic information to those with the technical expertise to resolve the problems, resulting in users' e-resource access issues being more effectively and expeditiously resolved. (37)

Training for coworkers can be accomplished in several different ways:

- library-wide staff orientation or onboarding process
- weekly or monthly e-mails targeted to certain library staff or even included in the library's staff-wide e-mails
- electronic documentation added on your library's problem report submission homepage or as additional web pages with useful reporting information in the form of FAQs
- face-to-face visits to relevant group staff meetings to answer their questions and offer on-the-spot additional training as needed

Training for coworkers should focus on the following topics:

- thorough descriptions of each facet of your library's problem reports: which facets are required, what they are, and how to capture them in a way that is relevant to a troubleshooter's information needs
- brief descriptions of your library's access chains and authentication methods: especially helpful if your library employs a discovery service, an access tool that may need further description because its behavior can often be bewildering to coworkers

Troubleshooting Your Troubleshooting Workflow

If you have an existing troubleshooting workflow, we hope this chapter has inspired you to consider possible improvements that could be made to better serve your patrons. At the same time, we realize how impractical some of our recommendations may seem if your current troubleshooting workflow is struggling. We recognize how overwhelming it can be to attempt to make improvements and, more so, to narrow your focus and prioritize which improvements should be made first. In this section, we highlight common pain points of troubleshooting workflows. Our number one recommendation for any pain point is to create documentation, if nothing else. Without documentation, you will spend more time either training (certain) staff or reiterating how to report issues to your coworkers than you have spent creating the documentation itself. Documentation created today saves time in the future. Otherwise, if you have identified several improvements that would benefit your troubleshooting workflow, work with your team leads to determine which single issue, if addressed, would make the greatest positive impact for the team—even if the solution will perhaps take effect after an extended period of hard work and dedication. Most issues do not have quick fixes, and it should be left up to leadership to determine where it is best to invest precious team resources. The following three questions are representative of common pain points of troubleshooting workflows:

- How should I advocate with library leadership to get additional staff resources for our troubleshooting team?
- How do I help troubleshooting team members improve their performance?
- If coworkers or frontline staff are reluctant to submit problem reports to the troubleshooting team, how can we improve our reporting rates?

QUESTION 1: HOW DO I ADVOCATE FOR ADDITIONAL STAFF?

If possible, delineate exactly how much time staff members currently spend on troubleshooting as well as why and how this is insufficient. The more numbers you are able to provide to library leadership, the better. For example, "John and I were able to close twenty-two help tickets last month. However, we were unable to adequately attend to sixty other help tickets that we received during the same time period." Be very clear about what, if any, other job duties are suffering due to the great amount of attention required by e-resource troubleshooting. Elucidate the customer service that is being provided to patrons by answering problem reports, how this is no different from the customer service offered at physical library service desks, and how this aligns with your library's or organization's strategic plan or goals. Formulate a staffing wish list before having a conversation with your leadership, and be prepared to make counteroffers. You could adjust your original request for a full-time staff member to a part-time staff member, a part-time staff member to a student assistant, or a student assistant to a few hours per week of an existing staff member's time. Reiterate how both patrons and library staff will be positively impacted if you are able to gain the additional staff for your troubleshooting team.

QUESTION 2: HOW DO I HELP TROUBLESHOOTING TEAM MEMBERS IMPROVE THEIR PERFORMANCE?

Solicit anonymized, individual feedback from team members about their frustrations, confusion, or need for more information on certain topics. Be sure to provide them the opportunity to submit open-ended responses. Also, consider that sometimes people "don't know what they don't know." Make the best decision you can as team lead to address the topics on which you think the team may need additional training. Then consider these steps:

- Use this feedback to revamp your documentation if necessary. Try documentation methods you have not previously employed, like screencast videos, blog posts, research guides, or other web pages.
- Add additional instructions or notes to some documents for particularly difficult issues. Your documentation may not have previously included any feedback from team members, but do not be afraid of the documents becoming too long or too literal. If a document helps one team member, it is likely that other members have had similar struggles and would also benefit from the same notes.
- Instate shadowing if this is not a part of your team's onboarding process.
- Heavily promote and foster authenticate group discussions. Even if for a while just leadership speaks at your team meetings, hopefully over time, others will feel more comfortable opening up and sharing with the group.
- Start a sort of show-and-tell at team meetings—if team members feel comfortable speaking to the group. At each meeting, team members can give a brief summary of what type of issues they have encountered since the team's previous meeting and bring up any topics they would like to discuss or gather more information on. In addition, team leads or trainers can also bring up relevant issues that they think would benefit from the group's attention.
- Proactively plan and schedule regular opportunities for continuing education. Preferably these sessions would provide extended time periods during which the entire team comes together for the sole purpose of learning. You can ask team members ahead of time which particular topics they would like covered during the event.

QUESTION 3: HOW DO I IMPROVE COWORKERS' AND FRONTLINE STAFF'S REPORTING RATES?

Although coworkers or frontline staff do not need a great amount of technical knowledge, they do need to know how to accurately report problems for both their own benefit and that of patrons. Oftentimes a lack of understanding of the significance of e-resource access issues causes library staff to underreport. As we have mentioned before, reporting itself can be seen as a burden. Even if you have already requested that staff report issues, with lackluster response, do keep trying, and consider mentioning the following when you next speak with your coworkers and frontline staff:

- We pay ___ amount each year for our e-resources; this represents ___ percent of our collections budget. We estimate that there are pervasive, ongoing access issues with ___ percent of our e-resources at any given time.
- The troubleshooting team is limited in what issues troubleshooters can proactively discover and greatly relies on problem reports to address existing issues. Coworkers and frontline staff members are in a prime position to discover e-resource access issues because they use e-resources prolifically while working with patrons.
- Please consider that if you, as a library staff member, are unlikely to report issues, how much more unlikely a patron is to report those very same issues. Patrons often have no idea that these issues can be reported, much less resolved. Also, patrons are often pressed for time and are willing to switch resources to get their information needs met. Library staff should take the time to report issues in case a future patron is unable to have an information need met by another resource.
- We understand how frustrating certain issues have been in the past when a resolution was not reached for several weeks. However, not all access issues are this severe or complicated. The bottom line is that we need to provide our patrons with access to our e-resources—no matter the time required to resolve an issue. We cannot even begin this process without first knowing about the issue.
- We take extra care to provide excellent customer service to our patrons who visit our physical service desks. Let's extend the same level of customer service to our online patrons. If you have found a broken link in your research travels, the probability is high that another patron has also found the same broken link and has not reported it.

In addition to these talking points, be sure to offer documentation of what is required of your reporters. Documentation with tips and tricks—such as how to capture a URL, where to find the necessary information to include in a problem report, and reminders about including adequate patron contact information—can be very helpful. If your library employs a discovery service, you may need to include some explanation of how it works alongside your reporting documentation. Often, coworkers and frontline staff members are overwhelmed and bewildered by how a discovery service behaves, leaving them with little concept of how many discovery service issues are not reproducible outside of the immediate moment of occurrence. Last, if there are only a few dissenters among your coworkers and frontline staff, reach out to them individually and really work with them on whatever their obstacles to reporting might be. They may not understand the reporting process and have been too embarrassed to ask for further clarification in a group setting. Especially if the dissenters are outspoken on issues without actually reporting them, a brief and respectful conversation with their supervisor may be necessary. Hopefully, overtime, a rapport will be built between the troubleshooting team and other library staff, with members of each side knowing that they can count on the others to do their part.

ADDITIONAL READINGS AND RESOURCES

American Society for Quality. 2020. "What Is a Flowchart?" Accessed April 8, 2020. https://asq.org/quality-resources/flowchart.

Bazeley, Jennifer. 2018. "Using LibGuides to Promote Communication between Public and Technical Services." In *Reengineering the Library: Issues in Electronic Resources Management*, edited by George Stachokas, 137–68. Chicago: ALA Editions.

Bazeley, Jennifer W., and Becky Yoose. 2013. "Technical Services Transparency: Using a LibGuide to Expose the Mysteries of Technical Services (Notes on Operations)." *Library Resources and Technical Services* 57 (2): 118.

Birrell, Lori, and Marcy A. Strong. 2018. "Creating Community: Drawing on Staff Expertise to Break Down Silos in Academic Libraries." *Collaborative Librarianship* 10 (2): 91–99.

Borchert, Carol Ann. 2006. "Untangling the Jungle of E-journal Access Issues Using CRM Software." *Library Collections, Acquisitions, and Technical Services* 30 (3/4): 224–37. doi:10.1080/14649055.2006.10766130.

Brown, Jennifer Everson. 2018. "Rethinking the Troubleshooting Model." *Journal of Electronic Resources Librarianship* 30 (4): 228–31. doi:10.1080/1941126X.2019.1593416.

Carter, Sunshine, and Stacie Traill. 2018. "Developing Staff Skills in E-resource Troubleshooting: Training, Assessment, and Continuous Progress." In *Reengineering the Library: Issues in Electronic Resources Management*, edited by George Stachokas, 233–52. Chicago: ALA Editions.

Daugherty, Alice, and Samantha Schmehl Hines. 2018. *Project Management in the Library Workplace*. Bingley, UK: Emerald.

England, Lenore, and Stephen D. Miller. 2015. *Maximizing Electronic Resources Management in Libraries: Applying Business Process Management*. Chandos Information Professional Series. Waltham, MA: Elsevier.

Ennis, Lisa A., and Randy S. Tims. 2012. "Help Central: Creating a Help Desk and Knowledge Portal in SharePoint." *Computers in Libraries* 32 (2): 6–10.

Erb, Rachel A., and Brian Erb. 2014. "Leveraging the LibGuides Platform for Electronic Resources Access Assistance." *Journal of Electronic Resources Librarianship* 26 (3): 170–89. doi:10.1080/1941126X.2014.939033.

Finch, Meghan. 2014. "Using Zapier with Trello for Electronic Resources Troubleshooting Workflow." *Code4Lib Journal* 26 (1). https://journal.code4lib.org/articles/10034.

German, Lisa. 2009. "No One Plans to Fail, They Fail to Plan: The Importance of Structured Project Planning." *Technicalities* 29 (3): 1–9.

Gould, Elyssa M. 2018. "Workflow Management Tools for Electronic Resources Management." *Serials Review* 44 (1): 71–74.

Hartnett, Eric, and Carole Thompson. 2010. "From Tedious to Timely: Screencasting to Troubleshoot Electronic Resource Issues." *Journal of Electronic Resources Librarianship* 22 (3–4): 102–12. doi:10.1080/1941126X.2010.535736.

Heaton, Robert. 2018. "Troubleshooting Personnel's Satisfaction with Software Tools." *Journal of Electronic Resources Librarianship* 30 (3): 119–30. doi:10.1080/1941126X.2018.1493977.

Hiatt, C. Derrik. 2015. "Technical Services Is Public Services." *Technicalities* 35 (5): 8–10.

Lambaria, Kate, Heidi R. Johnson, and Nicole Helregel. 2017. "Simulating Access Issues: Using Twine to Teach E-resources Troubleshooting." In *Teaching Technology in Libraries: Creative Ideas for Training Staff, Patrons and Students*, edited by Carol Smallwood and Lura Sanborn, 74–81. Jefferson, NC: McFarland.

Maddox Abbott, Jennifer A., and Mary S. Laskowski. 2014. "So Many Projects, So Few Resources: Using Effective Project Management in Technical Services." *Collection Management* 39 (2/3): 161–76. doi:10.1080/01462679.2014.891492.

Nawaz, Sabrina. 2016. "For Delegation to Work, It Has to Come with Coaching." *Harvard Business Review*, May 5, 2016. https://hbr.org/2016/05/for-delegation-to-work-it-has-to-come-with-coaching.

Porter, Seth. 2019. "Project Management in Higher Education: A Grounded Theory Case Study." *Library Management* 40 (5): 338–52. doi:10.1108/LM-06-2018-0050.

Resnick, Taryn. 2009. "Core Competencies for Electronic Resource Access Services." *Journal of Electronic Resources in Medical Libraries* 6 (2): 101–22.

Salas, Eduardo, Scott I. Tannenbaum, Kurt Kraiger, and Kimberly A. Smith-Jentsch. 2012. "The Science of Training and Development in Organizations: What Matters in Practice." *Psychological Science in the Public Interest* 13 (2): 74–101.

Searcy, Carly Wiggins. 2018. *Project Management in Libraries: On Time, On Budget, On Target.* Chicago: ALA Editions.

———. 2019. "Making a Plan for Project Success." *Technicalities* 39 (1): 1–6.

Stoddard, Morgan M., Bill Gillis, and Peter Cohn. 2019. "Agile Project Management in Libraries: Creating Collaborative, Resilient, Responsive Organizations." *Journal of Library Administration* 59 (5): 492–511. doi:10.1080/01930826.2019.1616971.

Swanberg, Kate. 2015. "The 12 Basic Principles of Agile Project Management." *Hubspot* (blog), January 5, 2015. https://blog.hubspot.com/agency/basic-principles-agile-project-management.

CASE STUDIES OF TROUBLESHOOTING WORKFLOWS

Beis, Christina A. 2018. "Simplifying E-resources Workflows with G Suite for Education." *Journal of Electronic Resources Librarianship* 30 (3): 161–63. doi:10.1080/1941126X.2018.1494091.

Christman, Dennis. 2018. "The New AskTech: Implementing a Ticketing System Platform for Technical Services Resource Troubleshooting." *Serials Review* 44 (3): 193–96. doi:10.1080/00987913.2018.1542765.

Coogan, John F. 2019. "E-resources Troubleshooting and User Support at a Primarily Distance Learning/Online Higher Education Institution: Current Practice and Future Considerations." *Journal of Electronic Resources Librarianship* 31 (3): 180–88. doi:10.1080/1941126X.2019.1635400.

Heaton, Robert. 2018. "Tools for Troubleshooting: Which Ones and What For." *Journal of Electronic Resources Librarianship* 30 (1): 9–26. doi:10.1080/1941126X.2018.1443903.

Kimbrough, John. 2018. "Technical Services and the Virtual Reference Desk: Mining Chat Transcripts for Improved E-resource Management." *Serials Librarian* 74 (1–4): 212–16. doi:10.1080/0361526X.2018.1428482.

Pan, Denise, Gayle Bradbeer, and Elaine Jurries. 2011. "From Communication to Collaboration: Blogging to Troubleshoot E-resources." *Electronic Library* 29 (3): 344–53.

Rathmel, Angela, Liisa Mobley, Buddy Pennington, and Adam Chandler. 2015. "Tools, Techniques, and Training: Results of an E-resources Troubleshooting Survey." *Journal of Electronic Resources Librarianship* 27 (2): 88–107. doi:10.1080/1941126X.2015.1029398.

Samples, Jacquie, and Ciara Healy. 2014. "Making It Look Easy: Maintaining the Magic of Access." *Serials Review* 40 (2): 105–17. doi:10.1080/00987913.2014.929483.

Wright, Jennifer. 2016. "Electronic Outages: What Broke, Who Broke It, and How to Track It." *Library Resources and Technical Services* 60 (3): 204–13.

EXAMPLE LIBRARY TROUBLESHOOTING RESEARCH GUIDES

Arthur Lakes Library at the Colorado School of Mines. 2020. "Off Campus Access: Troubleshooting Tips." Last updated March 18, 2020. http://libguides.mines.edu/offcampusaccess/troubleshooting.

Bowling Green State University Libraries. 2019. "Troubleshooting: Troubleshooting EZProxy and Access Problems." Last updated November 1, 2019. https://libguides.bgsu.edu/troubleshooting.

Charles L. Tutt Library at Colorado College. 2019. "Electronic Resources: Home." Last updated October 30, 2019. http://coloradocollege.libguides.com/Electronic Resources.

Colorado State University Libraries. 2020. "Electronic Resources: Troubleshooting . . . and Beyond." Accessed March 21, 2020. https://libguides.colostate.edu/eresources.

Freeman/Lozier Library at Bellevue University. 2017. "Troubleshooting Guide for Bellevue University Library: Database Troubleshooting." Last updated February 7, 2017. https://libguides.bellevue.edu/troubleshooting.

Hammermill and Ridge Libraries at Mercyhurst University. 2019. "Troubleshooting Online Library Resources: A Guide for Users: Login." Last updated October 18, 2019. https://library.mercyhurst.edu/friendly.php?s=troubleshoot.

Harriet K. and Philip Pumerantz Library at Western University of Health Sciences. 2020. "Electronic Resources Troubleshooting: Basic Troubleshooting." Last updated January 24, 2020. https://westernu.libguides.com/eresources_troubleshooting.

Leddy Library at the University of Windsor. 2020. "Access to the Library's Resources for Distance Education Students." Accessed March 21, 2020. http://leddy.uwindsor.ca/access-librarys-resources-distance-education-students.

Raymond H. Fogler Library at the University of Maine. 2018. "Troubleshooting Access to Online Resources: Common Issues." Last updated October 24, 2018. https://libguides.library.umaine.edu/troubleshooting.

Richard G. Trefry Library at American Public University System. 2020. "Technical Help Guide." https://apus.libguides.com/techhelp. Last updated January 6, 2020.

Shapiro Library at Southern New Hampshire University. 2019. "Troubleshooting Access to Library Resources." Last updated September 3, 2019. https://libguides.snhu.edu/troubleshooting.

Spokane Community Colleges Library. 2020. "Library Database Troubleshooting: Database Access Problems." Last updated March 11, 2020. https://libguides.scc.spokane.edu/troubleshooting.

University Library at California State University, Los Angeles. 2019. "Getting to Know E-resources." Last updated August 9, 2019. https://calstatela.libguides.com/erm.

University of Kansas Libraries. 2018. "Service Desk Resources: E-resources Troubleshooting." Last updated May 14, 2018. https://guides.lib.ku.edu/servicedesk/eaid.

University of Texas Libraries at the University of Texas at Austin. 2020. "Electronic Resources Troubleshooting." Last updated March 10. https://guides.lib.utexas.edu/ETS.

REFERENCES

Agile Alliance. 2020."12 Principles Behind the Agile Manifesto." Accessed April 8, 2020. www.agilealliance.org/agile101/12-principles-behind-the-agile-manifesto/.

Carter, Sunshine, and Stacie Traill. 2017. "Essential Skills and Knowledge for Troubleshooting E-resources Access Issues in a Web-Scale Discovery Environment." *Journal of Electronic Resources Librarianship* 29 (1): 1–15. doi:10.1080/1941126X.2017.1270096.

Collins, Maria, and Kristen Wilson. 2018. "An Agile Approach to Technical Services." *Serials Librarian* 74 (1–4): 9–18. doi:10.1080/0361526X.2018.1443652.

Hart, Katherine A., and Tammy S. Sugarman. 2016. "Developing an Interdepartmental Training Program for E-resources Troubleshooting." *Serials Librarian* 71 (1): 25–38. doi:10.1080/0361526X.2016.1169569.

Proactive Troubleshooting

Managing problem reports is a reactive process. Depending on an institu-tion's size and resulting number of library patrons, troubleshooters can quickly find themselves overwhelmed with the volume of problem reports they regularly receive. Staffing concerns can further compound the stress and chaos that can be caused by a high volume of problem reports. One of the avenues for attempting to reduce the number of problem reports received is to analyze your problem reports to identify systemic issues. Another is to conduct routine access checks for your library's holdings. Both of these proactive methods can be helpful in reducing both patron and librarian frustration. Analyzing your problem reports can reveal your library's most common issues, uncover previously unknown underlying issues, and help a troubleshooting team determine where they can course correct to better invest their limited resources. Conducting routine access checks can discover broken links before patrons are able to report them.

Proactive troubleshooting also encompasses working with access tool or e-resource vendors to address known issues via the vendor website, e-mail, phone, or in-person communication, as well as working with peer librarians whose libraries use similar products. Practicing proactive troubleshooting can potentially reduce your troubleshooting team's time spent reacting to issues and can be an effective way to get ahead of the deluge of tasks and technology issues that make up a troubleshooting workflow.

Analyzing Your Problem Reports

Troubleshooting workflows are, of course, designed with the best intentions, but gathering feedback or data after the workflow has been established for an extended amount of time can reveal valuable insights into how to make the work-flow more efficient and successful. Analyzing your problem reports can directly tie into workflow assessment because so many different variables can be evaluated against the troubleshooting team's assumptions or preconceived notions. Many libraries choose to analyze their problem reports with these goals in mind:

Identify systemic issues: Whether the systemic issues lie with particular e-resources, authentication methods, access tools, patron groups, or library staff members, some of them will lie undiscovered until troubleshooting team leadership is able to assess the entirety of problem reports received.

Determine if additional staffing resources are needed: Assessing problem report metrics like the amount of tickets received in a given time frame can help leadership advocate for additional staffing resources. Although sometimes skewed due to extenuating circumstances, the amount of time a problem report is unresolved can also be informative.

Assess quality control: Problem report analysis often reveals the level of customer service patrons are receiving, areas in which to develop continuing education for troubleshooting team members, and whether follow-up is being completed during an appropriate time frame.

Get buy-in from leadership: If previous efforts to demonstrate to your library's leadership the need for certain resources for your troubleshooting team have proved unsuccessful, collecting and organizing the quantitative data behind these requests may prove more successful. For example, if your troubleshooting team suffers particularly from the influx of problem reports received during exams, you could numerically illustrate this pain point to library leadership by comparing the average number of tickets received both during and outside of exam times.

Inform collection development: Details such as negative feedback on e-resources with limited seats, an extended number of downtimes due to vendor updates, or other resource features improperly functioning can all influence collection development decisions. Problem reports can provide valuable patron feedback that collection development librarians may not otherwise receive. Feedback can then be used to make collection development decisions. For example, if an egregious number of patrons is frequently denied access to an e-book with a limited number of simultaneous users, collection development staff may decide to buy more copies of the e-book.

In the Additional Readings and Resources at the end of this chapter, we include a Case Studies of Problem Report Analysis section. These articles include several different libraries that have examined and analyzed a certain number of their problem reports over a set time frame and have reported back their findings to readers. We recommend paying particular attention to libraries with similar staffing structures, e-resources, or access tools as your library.

If you decide to analyze your library's problem reports, we recommend analyzing a digestible time frame's worth, determining what variables you wish to confirm or deny ahead of time, developing a controlled vocabulary, and attempting to store any tag-like information within your problem reports. Think of tags that would be useful for your local needs. Consider labels such as authentication method, patron group, patron location, type of issue, or e-resource vendor. Example tags could include the following: on campus, off campus, staff, student, link failure, authentication issue, holdings error, or a particular vendor's name. Depending on your purposes, your problem reports could be sorted and categorized on the fly, by eye, but by storing the decisions made about what type of problem report a certain issue represents, you can prevent the work from being duplicated by others in the future. Similarly, using a controlled vocabulary of previously determined problem report descriptions can be beneficial, helping to prevent confusion among both current and future staff members who may have reason to review the analyzed problem reports in the future. Related to this, if more than one staff member will analyze your problem reports to categorize them with the tags you have decided on, be sure that these staff members are in agreement on tag definitions. Those who are responsible for analyzing the subset of problem reports may want to work on a few examples together to ensure agreement on categorizations.

Even if your troubleshooting team does not currently have the resources for a thorough examination of your problem reports, we hope that the considerations mentioned here will help you brainstorm what to look for during the limited amount of time you have to spend looking back over problem reports.

Access Checks

As libraries subscribe or purchase e-resources, a record of some sort is usually created that serves as a receipt for what exactly the library is gaining access to and for how long. These receipts could take the form of title lists from licenses, subscription agent interfaces, or vendor administration portals. Acquisitions records can also provide more details. Title lists from these sources usually include a title, a unique identifier (such as ISBN or ISSN), publisher or vendor information, coverage dates, and the website where the licensed content can be accessed. Subscription coverage dates vary widely from vendor to vendor, and libraries do not always maintain perpetual access to content they pay for. To determine whether the library retains perpetual access or post-cancellation access, the troubleshooter would need to consult the resource's specific license terms.

Although librarians do their best when cataloging their e-resources, technology complexities and acquisitions issues invariably produce inaccuracies in a library's holdings long after they were originally cataloged. Especially for e-journals, which experience title changes and publisher transfers, the very nature of subscriptions introduces many variables that may or may not cause your library's access to be inadvertently cut off. For example, acquisition payment issues arise when a vendor accidentally cuts a library's access even after payment was received or when a vendor forgets to reestablish access after dealing with a late payment from a library. One-time purchases can also experience similar acquisitions issues due to continuing access fees.

When conducting access checks, the goal is to compare a reliable access list, such as a vendor title list, to what has already been populated within your library's access tools. An access check for a single subscription ensures that the correct title, correct coverage dates, and correct platform for access are cataloged within your library's access tools and therefore available to patrons to discover. A vendor title list can be cross-referenced with acquisitions data when available, and acquisitions data alone can be used if a vendor does not provide a title list of subscriptions or one-time purchases. Different types of e-resources can have their access periodically checked at different times. Single-title subscriptions, such as e-journal and e-book packages, should probably be checked more often than one-time-purchase databases, e-books, and streaming videos. Large, aggregator databases do not need to be checked by individual titles because the content within them frequently changes. Jeffrey M. Mortimore and Jessica M. Minihan (2018) go into great detail about how often they conduct access checks for various types of e-resources and why. When prioritizing where to start when beginning e-resource access checks, consider the following:

Any known, systemic issues: For example, your library has received multiple problem reports that you are missing access to many titles on a single e-journal platform. Until you obtain a title list for the vendor platform, you will be unable to correct these issues en masse.

Your library's major vendors: For example, if the vast majority of your library's holdings are held between five to six vendors, it would be best to start with them.

Your library's most popular resources: Prioritize by subject discipline, audience size, or highest usage.

Any obvious discrepancies in what you should have access to and what you have cataloged: If you retrieve a title list for a publisher that states your library should have access to twenty titles but instead you have fifty titles cataloged, this should likely be examined sooner rather than later.

Although conducting access checks may seem like a daunting task, remember that this is a proactive process—your library simply doing what it can when it can is sufficient to meet the needs of its patrons. Spot-checking is also an alternative if your library does not have the staff time to devote to checking title lists, and so on, in their entirety. With limited staff time, a troubleshooter could check 20 percent of a library's holdings to determine if checking the remaining 80 percent is warranted. Not all title lists need to be checked individually in their entirety.

Troubleshooting Tip: Access Checks and Title Changes

Title changes are common with serials content, and there are various ways to deal with them according to the Anglo-American Cataloging Rules (or AACR2), RDA: Resource Description and Access, and your local cataloging policies. When reviewing title lists for access checks and verifying what is cataloged in your library's various access tools, do not be tempted to take shortcuts when dealing with title changes by simply editing the coverage dates on the most recent title of a journal. Track/represent/catalog each individual journal and its coverage dates within your link resolver, ERMS, MARC records, or elsewhere. Although e-journal access on a single web page is likely to encompass all title changes, some vendors use multiple web pages for the various titles. How exactly a vendor's website architecture accounts for title changes is not always obvious, and there may be unforeseen metadata issues when title changes are not properly cataloged. Each individual journal needs to be accounted for to ensure that OpenURL links work, interlibrary loan requests are able to be filled, and OCLC holdings are updated successfully.

Another remedy for limited staff time is to take advantage of any available link-checking features offered by your access tools. For example, Springshare offers an automated link-checking tool that libraries can use to find broken links in both LibGuides and LibGuides A–Z Database List. There are also other link-checking tools that you may be able to use at your library, such as Callisto (Headlee and Lahtinen 2014; Sharp Moon 2017) or SEESAU (Serials Experimental Electronic Subscription Access Utilities; Collins and Murray 2009). Even without link-checking tools, access checks can be conducted periodically by a staff member. Access checks are usually simple enough that they can be assigned to student workers or to any other staff members who are unfamiliar with e-resources. Generally, once shown the basic requirements of link checking, these staff members will succeed.

Troubleshooting Tip: Access Checks Can Trigger an IP Address Block

As you conduct access checks for your e-holdings, you may inadvertently trigger an IP address block by a vendor. For example, clicking into four different e-journals within a single minute may cause the vendor to read your activity as that of a robot or other text/data-mining software. Different vendors set different thresholds for what they consider suspicious activity, and not all vendors are quick to block an IP address. However, if you do encounter this issue, we recommend that you contact the vendor by both phone and e-mail, as this issue can sometimes be resolved quickly over the phone.

Working with Vendors and Peers to Proactively Troubleshoot

Some vendors periodically reach out to their customers for sales or other acquisitions purposes; they will often visit their customer libraries at least once a year, if not more often. If you are not the staff member who meets with your library's vendors, you can still connect with your coworkers who do in order to advocate for your patrons' needs. There are instances when certain e-resources have extended downtimes or lack certain desired technological features. Any qualms or grievances that library staff or patrons may have with a particular e-resource can be addressed at these periodic, face-to-face vendor meetings. Although some vendors place enhancement requests at a lower priority, many other vendors are happy and more than willing to receive such feedback from their customer libraries. They are often introducing features into their resources that require a great amount of feedback from end users to determine a new feature's worth. Vendors who are actively updating their existing e-resources, or developing new e-resources, would likely be very open to receiving feedback about their products. Circling back to extended downtimes—due to extenuating circumstances, some libraries have had success in advocating for a partial refund for their annual subscription rate if they experienced an unusual number of extended downtimes in a given time period. Periodic vendor meetings are one of the best venues for beginning such discussions. Outside of face-to-face meetings, reaching out to a vendor via e-mail to discuss these issues is also perfectly acceptable. Library acquisitions or licensing staff can make a recommendation on whether it is best to use a vendor's generic contact e-mail or, if the library has one, a dedicated customer service representative who could expedite and advocate on your library's behalf.

Similar to e-resource vendors, access tool vendors may also have established processes for customers who wish to advocate with technical support to implement fixes or enhancements to their products. This could take the form of the Ex Libris Idea Exchange, where customers have a limited number of votes to apply to user-submitted suggestions, or a standing meeting at a national conference, where issues are voted into priority ranking for the next system update. Some access tool vendors also provide electronic discussion lists for their customers to communicate with one another on issues. Examples include the following:

- EZPROXY-L@oclclists.org
- alma@exlibrisusers.org
- primo@exlibrisusers.org
- KB-L@listserv.oclclists.org
- eds_partners@ebscohost.com
- summon@exlibrisusers.org

Both regional library groups of consortia and professional electronic discussion lists, such as eril-l@lists.eril-l.org, can be great sources of proactive information when issues arise with common e-resource vendors. Many libraries will post to a list to inquire if other libraries with the same access tools or e-resources are experiencing the same issues at that time. Although you should still investigate and verify if an issue reported to an electronic discussion list is also occurring within your library's resources, sometimes it is very helpful to get ahead of an issue—possibly even before your patrons report it.

Another form of proactive troubleshooting is to advertise vendor downtimes or outages to your patrons via your library's homepage or access tools. Some vendors are very diligent about contacting their customers before planned outages or updates to their platforms. They might post the information on their websites and generally will also send this information to the e-mail address that they have on file as the main contact for your library. This is another example where it would be helpful to use a centralized e-mail address as your primary vendor contact, such as erteam@institution.edu, to ensure that the vendor updates are sent out to all relevant staff members. With the planned outage information in hand, you can then appropriately update your library's homepage or access tools with messages to your patrons about the dates and times of the outage. Be sure to also take advantage of customizable note features that may exist in your access tools for relaying this information to your patrons.

Conclusion

Proactive troubleshooting measures can both potentially reduce the number of problem reports received and help educate troubleshooting team leadership about where team resources are most needed. Analyzing help tickets can uncover previously unknown yet useful information for library staff beyond the troubleshooting team, such as collection development and acquisitions staff. Staffing resources have a direct impact on the volume of proactive troubleshooting that can be completed by a troubleshooting team. Some proactive troubleshooting measures, like access checks, can be completed by novice troubleshooters, such as student assistants and frontline staff. Outside of your library's troubleshooting workflow, vendors and peers are available to assist with proactive troubleshooting measures. Many vendors are eager to hear from their customers concerning either existing functionality improvements or enhancement requests. Peer libraries with similar e-resources or access tools are another source of support either by phone, e-mail, or posting to an electronic discussion list. Proactive troubleshooting requires a significant initial investment of troubleshooting team resources. However, the return on investment to the library's troubleshooting workflow in reducing both patron and library staff frustration is priceless.

ADDITIONAL READINGS AND RESOURCES

Ashmore, Beth, Emily Allee, and Rebekah Wood. 2015. "Identifying and Troubleshooting Link Resolution Issues with ILL Data." *Serials Review* 41 (1): 23–29.

Brûlé, Anne. 2009. "Troubleshooting Access to Electronic Resources." *Access* 15 (4): 12–13.

Bulock, Chris. 2015. "Techniques for Tracking Perpetual Access." *Serials Librarian* 68 (1–4): 290–98.

Donahoo, Nancy S., and Arthur Aguilera. 2019. "An Ongoing Treasure Hunt: One Library's Practical Experiences Documenting Post-cancellation Perpetual Access." *Serials Librarian* 76 (1–4): 83–85. doi:10.1080/0361526X.2019.1586234.

Emery, Jill, and Graham Stone. 2013. "Ongoing Evaluation and Access." *Library Technology Reports* 49 (2): 26–29.

Emery, Jill, Graham Stone, and Peter McCracken. 2020. "Troubleshooting." In *Techniques for Electronic Resource Management: TERMS and the Transition to Open*, 91–116. Chicago: ALA Editions.

Grissom, Andrew R., Steven A. Knowlton, and Rachel Elizabeth Scott. 2017. "Notes on Operations: Perpetual Access Information in Serials Holdings Records." *Library Resources and Technical Services* 61 (1): 57–62.

Mering, Margaret. 2015. "Preserving Electronic Scholarship for the Future: An Overview of LOCKSS, CLOCKSS, Portico, CHORUS, and the Keepers Registry." *Serials Review* 41 (4): 260–65.

Zhao, Wei, Shuzhen Zhao, and Katie-Scarlett MacGillivray. 2017. "Providing and Maintaining Access to Electronic Serials: Consortium and Member University Library's Perspectives." *Serials Librarian* 72 (1–4): 144–51. doi:10.1080/0361526X.2017.1309831.

CASE STUDIES OF PROBLEM REPORT ANALYSIS

Brett, Kelsey. 2018. "A Comparative Analysis of Electronic Resources Access Problems at Two University Libraries." *Journal of Electronic Resources Librarianship* 30 (4): 198–204. doi:10.1080/1941126X.2018.1521089.

Browning, Sommer. 2015. "Data, Data, Everywhere, nor Any Time to Think: DIY Analysis of E-resource Access Problems." *Journal of Electronic Resources Librarianship* 27 (1): 26–34. doi:10.1080/1941126X.2015.999521.

Enoch, Todd. 2018. "Tracking Down the Problem: The Development of a Web-Scale Discovery Troubleshooting Workflow." *Serials Librarian* 74 (1–4): 234–39. doi:10.1080/0361526X.2018.1427984.

Goldfinger, Rebecca Kemp, and Mark Hemhauser. 2016. "Looking for Trouble (Tickets): A Content Analysis of University of Maryland, College Park E-resource Access Problem Reports." *Serials Review* 42 (2): 84–97. doi:10.1080/00987913.2016.1179706.

Mann, Sanjeet, and Sarah Sutton. 2015. "Why Can't Students Get the Sources They Need? Results from a Real Electronic Resources Availability Study." *Serials Librarian* 68 (1–4): 180–90. doi:10.1080/0361526X.2015.1017419.

REFERENCES

Collins, Maria, and William T. Murray. 2009. "SEESAU: University of Georgia's Electronic Journal Verification System." *Serials Review* 35 (2): 80–87. doi:10.1016/j.serrev.2009.02.003.

Headlee, Patricia A., and Sandra C. Lahtinen. 2014. "Callisto." *Journal of the Medical Library Association* 102 (4): 305–6. doi:10.3163/1536-5050.102.4.018.

Mortimore, Jeffrey M., and Jessica M. Minihan. 2018. "Essential Audits for Proactive Electronic Resources Troubleshooting and Support." *Library Hi Tech News* 35 (1): 6–10. doi:10.1108/LHTN-11-2017-0085.

Sharp Moon. 2017. "Callisto." Accessed April 8, 2020. http://sharpmoon.com/callisto/.

CONCLUSION

Troubleshooting is an often-overlooked component of library customer service. Traditionally, libraries spend a great amount of time and energy cultivating the services and e-resources to meet patron information needs. However, librarians also need to ensure that these e-resources remain accessible throughout their life cycle. Establishing a strong troubleshooting workflow and staff, whose highest priority is customer service, is essential. With effective troubleshooting, a library can reduce patron frustration, foster a positive image of the library, increase the visibility of library services for patrons, and practice sound financial stewardship.

Throughout this book, we have covered several key concepts to improve both you and your library's troubleshooting skills. We discussed how troubleshooting is an extension of problem solving and that by defining and addressing the two problems of troubleshooting—the patron-focused problem and the technology-focused problem—a troubleshooter can both provide excellent customer service to patrons and address systemic technology issues. We also introduced the seven stages of problem solving that provide a troubleshooter with a road map to identify, diagnose, and resolve access issues. We then explored that road map, discussing the technical knowledge, strategic thinking, and problem-solving skills required for successful access issue resolution. Finally, we delved into how to troubleshoot a library's troubleshooting workflow, focusing on project management, training, and the workflow resources of staff, systems, technical skills, and time, before ending with proactive troubleshooting.

We hope after reading our book you feel better resourced as a troubleshooter by the new ideas, techniques, and concepts we have introduced. We also hope that you are inspired to embrace the inherent uncertainty of troubleshooting and feel confident enough to dive into the next access issue you encounter with newfound strength and resolve.

INDEX

f denotes figures; *t* denotes tables

#
4W1H questions, 41, 45–53
"12 Principles Behind the Agile Manifesto" (Agile Alliance), 125–126

A
The ABCs of ERM (Zellers, Adams, and Hill), 74
access chains
    authentication and, 21*f*, 22–25
    basic, 20–21
    comprehensive, 30–32*f*, 61*f*
    definition of, 13, 20
    for discovery interfaces, 27
    for discovery services, 29
    for knowledge bases, 28
    library services platforms and, 32–34
    library-controlled components of, 21, 60, 66*t*–67*t*, 71–73
    mapping questions for, 35
    patron-controlled components of, 21, 60–64, 66*t*–67*t*, 76, 91
    for research guides, 26–27
    vendor-controlled components of, 21, 60, 66*t*–67*t*, 73–74, 92–93
access checks, 157, 159–162
access issues
    diagnosing of (*see* diagnosing, process of)
    most common, 103*t*–106*t*
    resolution process for, 85–98
    types of problems in, 3–4
access tools
    in access chains, 20–21, 30–32*f*
    common issues with, 71–73
    customization of, 94
    definition of, 15
    metadata and, 67–68
    vendors of, 162–163
    See also specific tools
accountability, on teams, 130–133
acquisitions records, 77, 78, 81, 82, 105*t*, 107–108, 118, 160
Adams, Tina M., 74
advertising and marketing, 140
Agile Alliance, 125–126
agile project management, 125–128, 130, 134
Alma/Primo access chain, 32–34
application programming interfaces (APIs), 14, 66*t*
articles, problems accessing, 49–52, 79–81, 98–99, 112–116, 117–118
Asana, 135, 136
attitudinal competencies, 8–9
authentication
    in access chains, 20–26, 62–63
    definition of, 14
    via IP address, 22
    issues with, 78, 81, 82, 105*t*–106*t*, 120–123
    via proxy server, 22–23, 105*t*, 120–122
    via single sign-on (SSO), 25, 106*t*
    via username/password, 25, 106*t*, 122–123
    via virtual private network (VPN), 23–25, 106*t*
A–Z lists
    database, 16, 31*f*, 67*t*, 71–72, 75, 108, 111–112, 116–117
    e-journal, 16–17, 28, 31*f*, 67*t*, 70–71, 117–118, 120–122

B
backtracking, 7, 74, 75
big-picture issues, 94

binders, for documentation, 142
broken links. *See* links, broken
browsers
    in access chains, 22–26, 27*f*, 29*f*, 31*f*,
        61*f*, 63–65
    cache and cookies in, 14, 64–65, 78, 146
    common issues with, 64
    testing of, 65, 74–75
bullet journals, 131

C
caches, 14, 64–65, 78, 146
Callisto, 161
Carter, Sunshine, 8, 30, 32*f*, 141
catalogs (OPACs), 15, 19, 31*f*, 61*f*, 66*t*,
    116–117
central indexes, 16, 29–31*f*, 34, 61*f*, 66*t*, 69,
    88–89, 98
charters, 127–128
cognitive flexibility, 8, 9
cognitive psychology, 2, 20
collaboration, 125, 128–133, 141–147
collection development, informing, 158
communication, 94–98, 126, 132, 140
Community Zone, 32*f*, 34
competencies and skills, 6–9, 129
comprehensive access chains, 30–32*f*, 61*f*
CompTIA, 5
computer terminology, 14–15
contextual information, 40–41, 57
cookies, 14, 25, 64–65, 78, 146
coworkers, 129, 140, 147, 150–151
customer service culture, 10, 47–48, 97,
    133, 148, 150, 167

D
data mining, 106*t*
databases
    A–Z lists of, 16, 31*f*, 67*t*, 71–72, 75,
        108, 111–112, 116–117
    broken links to (*see* links, broken)
    of metadata (*see* knowledge bases
        (KBs))
    problems accessing, 54–55, 62,
        108–109, 110–112, 116–117,
        122–123
Davis, Susan, 88
DECSAR method, 5–6
devices, symptoms on, 63
diagnosing, process of
    access chains and, 59–64
    common symptoms in, 63–64, 71–74
    example scenarios of, 79–82
    for library-controlled components,
        71–73
    metadata and, 65–71
    for patron-controlled components,
        63–64

strategies for, 74–79
for vendor-controlled components,
    73–74
direct linking, 16
discovery interfaces, 16, 27, 66*t*, 107
discovery services, 16, 29–34, 66*t*, 69, 71,
    88–89, 112–115, 119
discussion lists, 79, 90, 163
documentation, 94–98, 136–142, 148, 149,
    150–151
domain-specific knowledge, 6–8

E
e-books, problems accessing, 109–110,
    119–120
EBSCO Discovery Service (EDS), 69
e-journals
    A–Z lists of, 16–17, 28, 31*f*, 67*t*, 70–71,
        117–118, 120–122
    problems accessing, 49–52, 79–81,
        98–99, 112–116, 117–118,
        120–122
    title changes of, 161
electronic discussion lists, 79, 90, 163
electronic resource management systems
    (ERMSs), 17, 28–29, 31*f*, 61*f*, 67*t*,
    70–71, 86
electronic resources librarians,
    competencies for, 9
electronic resources troubleshooting. *See*
    troubleshooting
elimination, 7, 64, 74–75
Emery, Jill, 74–75
enhancement requests, 162–163
Enoch, Todd, 42
e-resource implementation, incorrect, 104*t*,
    108–110
ERMSs (electronic resource management
    systems), 17, 28–29, 31*f*, 61*f*, 67*t*,
    70–71, 86
etiquette, professional, 47–48
Ex Libris, 34, 91, 162–163
external reporters, 40, 41–43, 45, 46,
    47–48
EZproxy, 15, 87–88, 91, 105*t*, 120–122, 163

F
films, problems accessing, 52–54, 81–82,
    99–101
follow-up, 95
frontline staff, 129, 140, 146–147, 150–151

G
general knowledge, 6–8
Google Scholar, 30, 31*f*, 61*f*
guiding principles, 126–128

H
half-splitting, 7, 74, 75–76
Hart, Katherine A., 43, 147
help tickets. *See* problem reports
Hill, Katherine, 74
holdings, incorrect, 70–71, 77, 81, 105*t*, 117–120
HTML, defined, 14
Huber, George, 1–2
hyperlinks
    broken (*see* links, broken)
    definition of, 15
    misdirecting, 71, 78, 104*t*–105*t*, 110–117

I
incognito mode, 65, 80
Institution Zone, 32*f*, 34
institutional repositories, 27, 29, 30, 31*f*, 61*f*
integrated library systems (ILSs), 17, 29, 31*f*, 61*f*, 66*t*. *See also* library systems
interlibrary loan, 48, 56, 88, 117–118, 119
internal reporters, 40, 42–43, 45, 48, 129, 150–151
internet protocol (IP) addresses
    authentication via, 22–25
    blocking of, 92, 162
    defined, 15
interviews, for troubleshooting, 45–56

J
Journal of Biology example, 49–50, 79–80, 98–99
Journal of Education example, 50–52, 80–81, 99
Journal of Electronic Resources Librarianship, 8
journals, problems accessing, 49–52, 79–81, 98–99, 112–116, 117–118, 120–122

K
knowledge, domain-specific, 6–8
knowledge bases (KBs)
    in access chains, 18, 28, 29, 31*f*, 34, 61*f*
    definition of, 17
    issues with, 86, 114, 115
    metadata and, 17, 28, 34, 66*t*–71
knowledge management systems
    in access chains, 20–21, 23*f*, 24*f*, 30–32, 35
    blended, 70–71
    definition of, 17
    See also specific systems

L
leadership, of teams, 127, 130–133, 141, 148–149

LibGuides, 16, 154, 161
librarians
    in access chains, 28*f*
    competencies and skills of, 6–9
    questionnaire for, 34–35
    troubleshooting interviews by, 45–56
    See also staff
libraries
    spheres of control held by, 21, 60, 66*t*–67*t*, 71–73
    terminology used in, 15–19
    types of problems at, 3–4
    websites of, 26, 27*f*, 29*f*, 31*f*, 61*f*, 71–72
library services platforms (LSPs), 17, 18, 32–34, 67*t*, 99, 114, 115–116
library systems
    access chains in (*see* access chains)
    importance of understanding, 13
    LSPs as next generation of, 17, 18, 32–34, 67*t*, 99, 114, 115–116
    mental models of, 20, 34–35
    questionnaire on, 35
    terminology for, 14–19
link resolvers, 8, 18, 31*f*, 61*f*, 67*t*, 70–71, 80, 141
link-checking tools, 161
links, broken
    common reasons for, 104*t*–105*t*
    example scenarios of, 3–4, 41–42, 49–50, 79–80, 88–89, 110–117
    first steps when encountering, 78
    incorrect metadata and, 68–69, 104*t*
    link-checking tools for finding, 161

M
MARC records, 19, 66*t*, 67*t*, 69, 117
Mayer, Richard E., 2, 8
McCracken, Peter, 74–75
mental models, 20
metadata
    incorrect and faulty, 65, 67–68, 98, 104*t*
    sources and types of, 65–69
    spheres of control for, 21, 65–67*t*
Minihan, Jessica M., 160
mission statements, 127, 128
morale, 132–133, 144
Mortimore, Jeffrey M., 160
motivation, in problem solving, 3, 8, 9

N
network connections, slow, 63
Network Zone, 34
North American Serials Interest Group (NASIG), 9
note taking, 145

O

objectives, in problem solving, 2–3
obstacles, in problem solving, 2–4, 8
online catalogs (OPACs), 15, 19, 31*f,* 61*f,*
    66*t,* 116–117
OpenURL, 8, 16, 18*f,* 113, 141
Orr, R. Robert, 5–6
out-of-the-box solutions, 94

P

pain points, 134, 148–151
patrons
    as external reporters, 40, 41–43, 45, 46,
        47–48
    problem solving focused on, 2–4, 40,
        107–111, 112–121, 123, 133–
        134, 137*f*–139*f*
    spheres of control held by, 21, 60–64,
        66*t*–67*t,* 76, 91
    user error by, 4, 54–57, 103*t*
paywalls, 50–52, 70–72, 77, 78, 80, 99,
    105*t*
permalinks, 15, 49–50. *See also* hyperlinks
platforms, defined, 15
Practical Problem Solving for Managers
    (Stevens), 2
Primo, 32–34, 69, 163
Primo Central Index (PCI), 32*f,* 34
problem reports
    analysis of, 157–159, 165
    basics of, 39–41
    challenges with, 41–45
    common issues with, 103*t*–106*t*
    example scenarios of, 48–57
    external reporters of, 40, 41–43, 45, 46,
        47–48
    internal reporters of, 40, 42–43, 45, 48,
        129, 150–151
    staffing considerations for, 129
    submission forms for, 43–44*f*
    systems for managing, 134–135
    troubleshooting interviews and, 45–56
problem solving
    definitions of, 1–3
    patron-focused, 2–4, 40, 107–111,
        112–121, 123, 133–134,
        137*f*–139*f*
    of reproducible *vs.* unreproducible
        problems, 60–63
    stages of, 4–6, 39, 85
    technology-focused, 3–4, 40, 137*f*–139*f*
    See also troubleshooting
project charters, 127–128
project management, 125–128, 130, 134
proxy servers
    in access chains, 22–23, 26–27*f,* 29*f,*
        31*f,* 61*f*

authentication via, 22–23
definition of, 15
issues with, 62–63, 70–73, 87–88, 105*t,*
    120–122
stanzas for, 91, 105*t,* 122

Q

questions
    for mapping library systems, 35
    for problem reports, 41, 45–53
    for troubleshooting workflows,
        148–151

R

Rashomon example, 52–54, 81–82, 99–101
re-creation, 7, 60–63, 74–76
reference interviews, 45
reflection, 130–131
reports. *See* problem reports
reproducible *vs.* unreproducible problems,
    60–63
research guides
    in access chains, 26–27, 31*f,* 61*f*
    definition of, 19
    issues with, 71–72, 75, 110–111,
        120–121
    metadata in, 67*t*
    on troubleshooting, 92, 154–155
resolutions, working toward, 85–98
results, reviewing of, 5, 6, 85, 93
Ross, Craig, 5–6

S

scope, defining, 78–79
screencast videos, 143
SEESAU, 161
self-reflection, 130–131
servers, defined, 15. *See also* proxy servers
Shapiro Library, 92
single sign-on (SSO), 15, 25, 106*t*
skills and competencies, 6–9, 129
Slack, 135, 136
Smith, Mike U., 40
solutions, working toward, 85–98
source records, 69
Southern New Hampshire University, 92
spheres of control, 21, 60–67*t,* 71–74
split tunneling, 24–25, 106*t*
Springshare, 16, 161
SSO (single sign-on), 15, 25, 106*t*
staff
    advocating for, 148–149
    base knowledge of, 125, 129
    competencies and skills in, 6–9, 129
    as coworkers, 129, 140, 147, 150–151
    on the frontlines, 129, 140, 146–147,
        150–151

improving the performance of, 149
increasing reporting by, 150–151
labeling members of, 128–129
morale of, 132–133, 144
robust *vs.* lean levels of, 10
training of, 141–147
See also teams

stanzas, 73, 87, 91, 105*t*, 122
Stevens, Michael, 2
Stone, Graham, 74–75
submission forms, 43–44*f*
Sugarman, Tammy S., 43, 147
symptoms, common, 63–64, 71–74
systems. *See* library systems

T
teams
    documentation by, 136–142
    guiding principles for, 126–128
    improving the performance of,
        149–151
    labeling members of, 128–129
    leadership of, 127, 130–133, 141,
        148–149
    problem reports and, 134–135,
        150–151
    training of, 141–147
    See also staff
technology terminology, 14–19
technology-focused problem solving, 3–4,
    40, 137*f*–139*f*
title changes, 161
Traill, Stacie, 8, 30, 32*f*, 141
training, 141–147
triage situations, 96–98
trial and error, 7
troubleshooting
    access chains in (*see* access chains)
    diagnoses in (*see* diagnosing, process
        of)
    example scenarios of, 48–57, 79–82,
        98–101, 107–123
    importance of, vii
    infrastructure for, 9–11
    knowledge necessary for, 6–9
    mental models for, 20
    proactive, 157–164
    as problem solving, 1–6
    reports for (*see* problem reports)
    resolutions in, 85–98
    stages of, 4–6, 39, 85
    strategies for, 7, 74–78
    terminology in, 14–19
    tips for, 65, 69, 73, 87, 91, 93, 140,
        161–162
    workflows for (*see* workflows)
troubleshooting interviews, 45–56

U
University of Minnesota, 30, 32*f*
University of Texas Libraries, 92
unreproducible *vs.* reproducible problems,
    60–63
URLs (uniform resource locators)
    defined, 15
    issues with, 72–73, 75, 78, 105*t*
    See also hyperlinks
user error, 4, 54–57, 103*t*
username/password authentication, 25,
    106*t*, 122–123

V
vendors
    in access chains, 21–29, 31*f*, 34–35,
        60–61*f*
    administration portals of, 77, 79, 93,
        98–99, 159
    common issues with, 104*t*–107
    IP address blocking by, 92, 162
    paywalls from, 50–52, 70–72, 77, 78,
        80, 99, 105*t*
    proactively working with, 162–164
    representatives from, 92–93, 100
    spheres of control held by, 21, 60,
        66*t*–67*t*, 73–74, 92–93
    username/password authentication
        from, 25, 106*t*, 122–123
videos
    problems accessing, 52–54, 81–82,
        99–101
    for troubleshooting training, 143
virtual private networks (VPNs), 15, 23–25,
    62–63, 106*t*

W
WAYF menu, 25, 76, 106*t*
websites
    library, 26, 27*f*, 29*f*, 31*f*, 61*f*, 71–72
    verifying if down, 73
workflows
    accountability in, 130–133
    case studies of, 153
    designing of, 133–140
    documentation in, 136–142
    flowcharts of, 136–139*f*
    infrastructure and, 9–10
    pain points in, 134, 148–151
    project management and, 125–128,
        130, 134
    staffing considerations for, 128–129
    teams for (*see* teams)
    training in, 141–147

Z
Zellers, Jessica, 74